aloha
veggies

aloha veggies

Veg-Forward Recipes Celebrating the Flavors of Hawaiʻi

Alana Kysar

Photography by Alana Kysar

Artwork by Moses Aipa

Also by Alana Kysar: *Aloha Kitchen*

TEN SPEED PRESS

California | New York

Mauna Kahālāwai, Maui

To Hawai'i, a place I am grateful beyond measure to call home. To all who tend the 'āina, mahalo for nurturing the land that fills us all with aloha.

contents

starches

O.K. Farms, Hilo, Hawaiʻi Island

aloha, veggies

Aloha means so much: It's love, hello, goodbye. It's a feeling and a way of life. But in this instance, let's say, "Aloha, Veggies," as in, "Hello, Veggies!"

Returning home to Maui at the beginning of 2022 meant rediscovering a lot about the island where I grew up—and of course, the revelations began in the kitchen. The island I grew up on was both familiar and new to me. While I spent my first eighteen years on Maui, I had not lived here in my adulthood, so in many ways my homecoming was not only about refamiliarizing myself with the island, but in part exploring a new, somewhat different home. I was pleasantly surprised to discover a renewed agricultural scene on the island and in Hawai'i at large, ostensibly in response to the rising need to source food locally rather than rely on unstable imports. This has always been the case in Hawai'i, but the global pandemic made this more apparent and urgent.

I was born and raised in Hawai'i and grew up in Kula, a small city on the slopes of Haleakalā, Maui's largest volcano, and have returned to the same neighborhood that was the backdrop for all my childhood memories. However, even the drive home looks different. Haleakalā Highway, the long road up the mountain once seemingly paved between the sugarcane, is now lined with rows of citrus trees, coffee plants, and other new crops. HC&S, Hawai'i's last sugarcane producer, ended sugar production and operations on Maui in 2016, freeing up over 36,000 acres of agricultural land for local food production. Today, there are swaths of new crops being farmed on what was once sugarcane land. As an adult, I look at Maui through a new lens and pay attention to different things. Where I was once concerned with the fastest route to Big Beach in Makena, I am now slowing down to take in the sights, soaking in how the drive looks and feels. Nowadays, I find myself taking the long way, stopping to admire the majestic beauty of the land. Maui is home to over eight hundred farms primarily focused on produce, growing everything from breadfruit ('ulu) and taro (kalo) to parsnips and citrus. And I'm pretty sure my twelve-year-old self was not invested in what was being grown on the island, but now I'm always looking around to see what's growing and where.

The USDA's 2022 Census of Agriculture reported 6,569 crop and livestock farms statewide here in Hawai'i. I expect (and hope for) that number to skyrocket in the coming years. Following the devastating fires on Maui in 2023, I've seen an increased push for local food production through community interest in locally sourced food, an uptick in grants to increase local food production, and businesses looking for ways to support local farms to promote growth. In 2024, the popular plate lunch chain L&L Hawaiian Barbecue partnered with Hawai'i 'Ulu Cooperative to offer Hawai'i-grown taro and sweet potato ('uala) as a healthier, locally sourced alternative to rice or mac salad at their Hawai'i locations.

The idea of contributing a new lexicon of vegetable deliciousness to the local food culture in a significant way and providing valuable

Kula, Maui

tools to our community is something that really speaks to me. Shortly after we moved home, my husband and I had an incredible meal at Lineage, a restaurant in Wailea, Maui, centered around cooking with local ingredients and many veg-forward dishes. I thought to myself, We need more of this here. They had a dish called Bird's Nest that featured oyster mushrooms (from a farm in Olinda called Lapa'au Farm), bok choy, eggplant, and other seasonal veggies served atop a bed of crispy fried taro with a gravy that was familiar (think cake noodle) but different that I still think about. On O'ahu, Chef Ed Kenney has been doing amazing things with local produce for decades, first at Town and now at Mud Hen Water. Moon and Turtle in Hilo on Hawai'i Island had an incredible dish they called Drunken Mushrooms, which featured Hāmākua ali'i mushrooms (also known as king trumpets) and charred cabbage; I still salivate just thinking about it. Looking around, I started to see that the community in general, not just the restaurant industry, was starting to champion locally grown produce. A farm from my favorite Maui farmers' market, Upcountry Farmers Market, opened up a beautiful brick and mortar selling not just their produce but produce from farmers all over the island and value-added goods made with locally sourced produce like breadfruit hummus.

After living in California for almost a decade, I was reminded of the meat-centric nature of local island cuisine upon my return. Although I'm an enthusiastic omnivore, I found myself craving the abundance of vegetables found on menus and in home kitchens that feature Californian and other cuisines in Los Angeles and San Francisco. Seeing the exciting way a few local restaurants were bringing vegetables to the forefront, I began to dream about using the flavors and techniques I grew up loving in local Hawai'i food to create a cornucopia of vegetable-forward meals. The more I explored this idea, the more I realized that local Hawai'i cuisine's familiar tastes, methods, and textures are ideally suited for vegetable- and plant-based cooking. Enter: *Aloha Veggies*.

Two of the most frequent complaints I hear from home cooks—no matter where they live—are, "I don't know how to cook vegetables" and "How do you make vegetables taste good?" In the context of local Hawai'i food, a majority of the dishes that we cherish revolve around a protein, such as pork or chicken, but this does not mean that the flavors and cooking methods cannot be modified for vegetables and similar ingredients. Vegetables are so diverse—much more than meat, in textures, tastes, and so on—that making them taste good is easy. When you pick the right vegetable for the dish, you will be amazed by what you can create. For example, if you want something that's both meaty and chewy, try oyster or king trumpet mushrooms. If you want something creamy and sweet when roasted, look no further than a Honeynut or kabocha squash.

Historically, vegetables have not been the center of the plate in Hawai'i, but a lot of that is because of accessibility. Nowadays, we have access to a wider variety of produce that was previously harder to come by. As we move forward as a community, we'll likely reevaluate our new normal, with an increased need and desire to incorporate more locally sourced ingredients. I have a small backyard garden on the slopes of Haleakalā, where I grow a diverse range of produce, including five types of squash, plenty of herbs, different varieties of tomatoes, bush beans, and eggplants. My friends are growing mushrooms nearby, thousands of people share backyard gardening tips in local Facebook groups that do monthly produce swaps, and grocery stores are newly committed to purchasing and highlighting locally grown food. Our local farmers' markets are a sight to behold: all the colors of the rainbow with a wide range of produce that would rival the very best farmers' markets of California. I believe it's time for us to embrace vegetable-focused cooking in Hawai'i and worldwide.

The purpose of this book is not to advocate for vegetarianism or claim that cooking with vegetables is inherently healthier. I aim to use familiar flavors in new and exciting ways, explore techniques rooted in local Hawai'i cooking, and incorporate fresh ingredients. Hawai'i's local food culture was built by and primarily influenced by the three major diasporas that ended up in Hawai'i, so it encompasses Hawaiian dishes like poi, made from baked and pounded taro, as well as hearty braised meats, stews, and stir-fries from Chinese, Japanese, Portuguese, Korean, and Filipino settlers. I firmly believe that vegetables can take center stage in a meal, and my goal is to showcase how to build satisfying and complete meals around them, making a positive change in our diets, not only for our bodies but also for our communities and the planet.

Before starting this project, my husband and I ate meat four or five days a week for at least one meal, sometimes two. Since I wrote the book, our diets have changed dramatically. This isn't to say we aren't eating a steak or some kālua pig now and then, because we are. However, for the most part, we now eat pretty veg-forward. And here's what I want to say about this. I've struggled with veg-forward eating, mostly because I never felt full. So when I was developing these recipes, that was very important to me. Whenever friends came over for recipe test meals, at the end of every meal, I asked, "Are you full?" I have struggled for years to find a good balance when crafting veg-forward meals. I created the basic formula of this book with that in mind. And to answer my question, yes, now we are always full after our veggie-filled meals!

Making food that leaves you feeling full was one part of my mission, but the other was a little more nuanced and equally, if not more, important to me. It's my goal to contribute to the ever-evolving category that is local Hawai'i food. Local cuisine reflects what the locals in Hawai'i eat and is imbued with nostalgia, as each dish represents a unique food memory. Whenever I smell mochiko chicken, a sweet and salty fried chicken, I am instantly transported to my elementary school field trips, my mom's kitchen, and my childhood. However, because these dishes are passed down through families, each family has their spin on a dish. For example, I recently discovered a new recipe for pohole fern salad that includes ingredients different from the one I grew up with. Still, I think both versions are equally delicious and embody the dish's essence. I believe there is always room for innovation and adaptation in cooking. With the recent increase in the diversity of local agriculture, we have access to a wide variety of produce that can be incorporated into our local cuisine. Let's embrace these new ingredients and continue evolving our food culture while honoring our traditions.

This book embodies the way that I cook local Hawai'i food at home. Like all family recipes, it might differ from a recipe you know and love, but it's how I cook my heritage today. It's not traditional; it could be called a modern interpretation of a dish or flavor. However, as I explored in my debut cookbook, *Aloha Kitchen*, like many family recipes, these veg-forward recipes are rooted in Hawai'i's local food culture. The recipes in this book are a compilation of my past and present life and, hopefully, our future. My hope and goal have always been that my recipes can become yours and that you take them as a guide to create your family recipes to pass down to future generations.

When I first set out to write this book, my mom, a sansei, or third-generation Japanese American, born and raised in Hilo on Hawai'i Island, was skeptical at best. She, like most people who grew up here, grew up eating meals centered around meat. When I told her that I wanted to write an entire book that focused on vegetables, taking the flavors and dishes she already knows and loves, but making them veg-forward, well, she was less than enthusiastic. She essentially told me she didn't think anyone would be interested in it. So I made it my mission to prove that she might love some of the dishes. I'd tell her what I was making, "Oh, Mom, I'm making Miso Beets with Cannellini Beans." And I'd usually be met with something like, "Hmmm, that sounds interesting." But the subtext was more like, "Hmm, that's different." Or "Hmm, I'm not sure I'll like that." So I'd drop off a sample when it was done to get her opinion. She'd text me her thoughts, usually in a few words or less. I believe I got a "Great" in response to that dish, which was a huge surprise. Of course, they weren't all wins; I did get some "Fine"s. But I will say that there were more wins than losses. And mostly winning over my mom was kind of everything.

While most of these recipes look new or different from what you're accustomed to, they should all taste familiar and comforting. And that's the end goal here. To take a flavor you know and love and pair it with the right vegetables to let the veggie and the essence of that nostalgic dish shine. Doing it several times sets you up to find more combos and preparations that speak to you. Finding different ways to capture the essence of food memory or flavor sets you up to cook more veggies. I won over my mom; now I'm hoping to win you over, too, with these simple and delicious recipes. I, a home cook, wrote them for you to cook in your home. They're meant to be joyous and fresh, familiar, and fun!

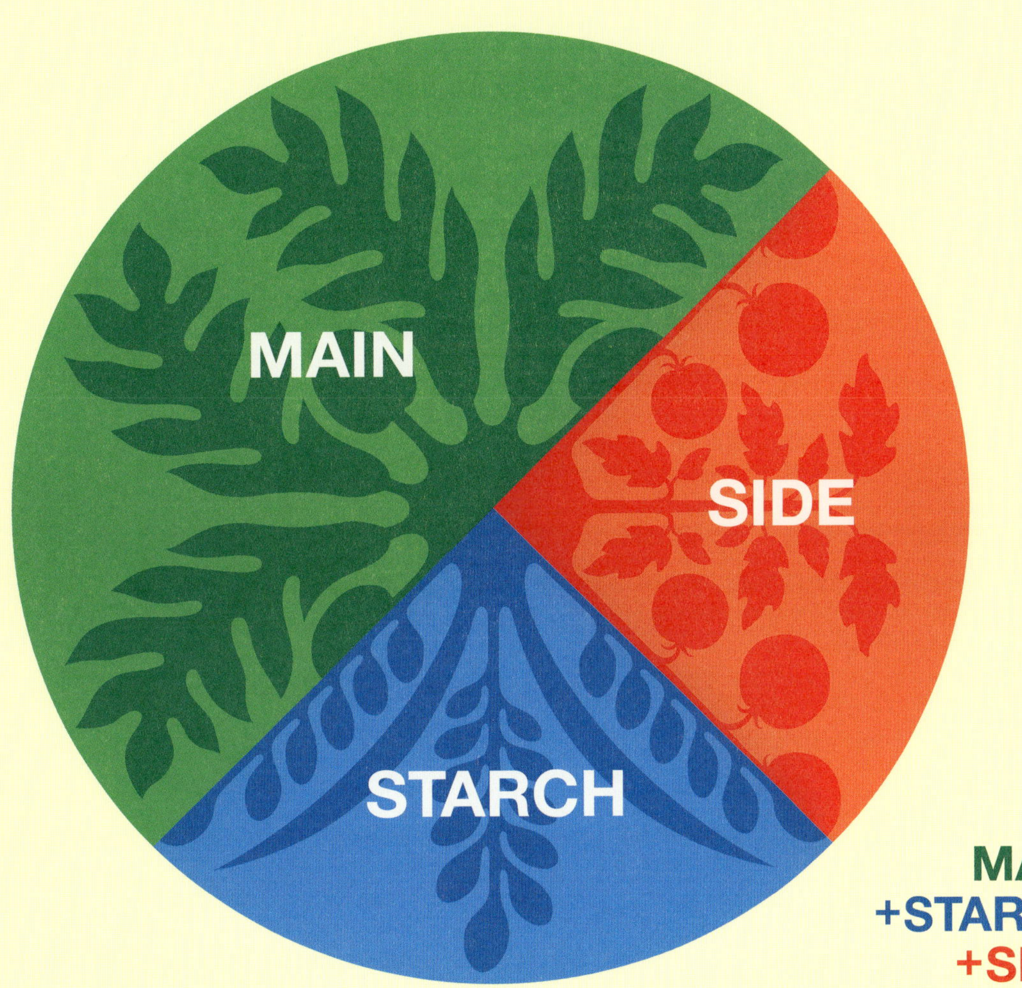

MAIN
+STARCH
+SIDE

COMPLETE MEAL

the plate lunch

These days, the plate lunch is nearly synonymous with Hawai'i and, more specifically, local Hawai'i food. The structure of a plate lunch is generally easy to break down: It's a plate usually filled with (1) a protein (think chicken katsu, pork laulau, or beef stew), (2) a starch (almost always white rice, sometimes hapa rice, which is a combination of white and brown rice), and (3) a mayo-y starch like mac salad and/or a veggie like a tossed salad or something pickled like kimchi. Stripped down, this formula can be applied to most meals. *Aloha Veggies* elaborates on this idea with an organized structure of chapters focusing on the key components of a plate lunch and recipe subchapters exploring familiar flavors and techniques and variations therein.

This book's fundamental equation for a complete meal is "Main + Starch + Side = Complete Meal." Additionally, you can opt to add a sweet as a bonus. The goal is to create simple systems for easy, everyday meals that are nutritious, vegetable-packed, and satisfying rather than just being considered health foods. There's nothing worse than finishing your meal and feeling hungry. I have built these dishes to be paired together to leave you feeling satisfied at the end of your meal. The serving sizes are meant to be a guide and are built around the meal equation. This isn't to say that some recipes can't stand alone; they absolutely can. However, when looking at a serving size, assume that to serve *x* number of people, you need to make a main, a starch, and a side.

how to use this book

The structure of this book may look a little different from others you've seen in the past, but once you familiarize yourself with it, it's easy to use! I was inspired by Amy Chaplin's *Whole Food Cooking Every Day*, wherein Chaplin divided the book into twenty chapters, each containing a base recipe and some variations. In *Aloha Veggies,* you'll find your standard chapters like Mains, Starches, and Sides, and yes, there's a Sweets chapter, too. But within each of these chapters are subchapters, each with four recipe variations inspired by one particular dish, flavor, or method.

What I aim to do is equip you with an arsenal of recipes that explore ways to adapt familiar favorites to a broader range of veggie-forward ingredients or combinations! For example, in Mains, Shoyu is a subchapter, and within that subchapter, you'll find four recipes that are inspired by the flavors of shoyu chicken: Shoyu Cauliflower with Chickpeas (page 25), Shoyu Kabocha with Green Onion Oil and Whipped Tofu (page 26), Shoyu-Roasted Carrots with Butter Bean Puree (page 29), and Shoyu Japanese Turnips with Oyster Mushrooms and≈Bok Choy (page 30).

The idea is that familiar local dishes and flavors lend themselves to many interpretations. As you'll find with local Hawai'i food, simple techniques and methods yield delicious and flavorful dishes. Once you cook a few versions, you can endlessly adapt these dishes to what you have on hand. My hope is that *Aloha Veggies* will ignite excitement for the limitless possibilities of vegetable cooking and inspire a new generation of home cooks in Hawai'i and beyond to create their own recipes using ingredients readily available and maybe even locally grown. This structure lets you consider what flavor you're craving and find a few options for that specific flavor profile. Maybe you're craving miso. Well, there are four miso-packed mains to contemplate!

READ AND THEN REREAD

This book is all about everyday cooking for everyday people. I wrote this book for us, the people who want delicious, satisfying meals but don't necessarily want to spend all day in the kitchen. While there are bound to be some exceptions, expect these recipes to be straightforward. That being said, please, pretty please, read each recipe over from start to finish, then reread it before you get started. Not only will you familiarize yourself with the steps before you dive in, but you'll also be able to inventory your pantry, fridge, counter, etc., and figure out how much time you'll need to finish a dish.

TOOLS

These tools might be outside your everyday staples like a Dutch oven, knives, saucepan, small frying pan (skillet), large skillet, spatulas, etc., and might need further explanation or examination.

Microplane: A rasp-style grater that can grate garlic and ginger, zest citrus, and finely grate hard cheese. I'd call it a must-have, so if you don't have one, I'd suggest adding it. You'll use it all the time.

Quarter-sheet and half-sheet pans: These rimmed baking sheets should already be in your everyday tool kit. A quarter-sheet measures 13 by 9 inches and a half-sheet measures 18 by 13 inches.

Rice cooker: We have invested heavily in our rice cooker and have a Zojirushi Pressure Induction Heating Rice Cooker & Warmer NP-NWC10. However, I'd recommend just about any Zojirushi model.

Sesame grinder: This is not necessarily a must-have but an excellent tool for grinding/crushing sesame seeds. You can get a fancy battery-powered grinder or a little plastic hand-crank grinder; both work well.

Steamer basket: The recipes in this book were written for bamboo and metal steamer baskets that rest atop a pot. If you're using a metal steamer that fits internally in the pot, adjust water levels accordingly and check the water level through the steaming process to ensure all the water hasn't evaporated.

knife cuts
(& grating)
These are the basic cuts called for in the book.
MINCE
Cut into very small pieces, smaller than a grain of rice
CHOP
Cut into small bite-size pieces (around ¼ inch); roughly the same size
DICE
Cut into ½-inch cubes
CUBE
Cut into ¾-inch cubes
ROUGH CHOP
Cut into large, somewhat irregular pieces (around ¾ inch)
THINLY SLICE ON A BIAS
Long, diagonal slices, usually green onions
THINLY SLICE
Long slices, from pole to pole, usually sweet onions
JULIENNE
Cut into thin matchstick-like pieces
FINELY JULIENNE
Really thin matchsticks, usually ginger
SHRED
Cut into thin strips, usually leafy greens
GRATE
Use the small holes on a box grater
FINELY GRATE
Use a rasp-style grater like a Microplane

happy HOLIDAYS
CANCEL
MENU
START
REHEAT
TIMER
PRESSURE IH

for the love of rice:

an ode to the rice cooker

When I was growing up in Hawai‘i, almost every meal started and ended with rice. Breakfast was often scrambled eggs, cheesy eggs if I was lucky, and fluffy steamed white rice. Lunch consisted of lots of bentos with musubi and teri sticks. And dinner was always a main served with a side of rice. Steamed white rice has always reigned supreme in my life and in most homes here in Hawai‘i. Most local Hawai‘i dishes are served alongside a mound of fluffy rice and a side—or often with only rice.

The earliest wave of Chinese workers started Hawai‘i's long love of rice. Chinese immigrants wanted rice instead of the poi made from taro (kalo) that could be found. This led to taro patches being turned into rice paddies due to their similar need for lots of water. Rice production ramped up in the late 1800s and, at one point, became the second-largest crop in Hawai‘i. It later declined partly due to competition from mainland growers and preferences for different types of rice, namely short-grain or medium-grain, rather than the long-grain being grown locally. The last remaining rice mill in Hawai‘i is a nonprofit agrarian museum called Ho‘opulapula Haraguchi Rice Mill, located within a kalo farm called Hanalei Taro in Hanalei Valley on the island of Kaua‘i.

If you're from Hawai‘i, chances are good that you grew up cooking rice. And by cooking rice, I mean you learned how to cook rice in a rice cooker. We love rice! In some cultures, bread is always on the table; in Hawai‘i, you always have a pot of rice on standby. It wasn't until my adulthood that I learned how to cook rice on the stovetop, and I failed miserably the first few times. To be fair, longer grains like basmati and jasmine are relatively easy to cook on the stovetop, but the rice we love in Hawai‘i, medium- and short-grain rice, is somewhat tricky to nail on the stovetop. And while I understand the urge to dismiss the need for another appliance in your kitchen, if you eat rice with most meals, I think a rice cooker is a necessity. Work smarter, not harder.

I'd go as far as to say I almost love my rice cooker. My rice is always perfect: tender, a little chewy and moist (never mushy), and my rice cooker even sings me a little song when the rice is ready. I've raved about it to friends, family, and even Buy Side from the *Wall Street Journal*. So here's why I (almost) love my rice cooker. Rice cookers cook better rice! Since it's their primary job, they are made to maintain the proper balance of steam and heat throughout the cooking process to cook your rice as well as it can be cooked. That means you'll get the most out of each kernel: flavor, tenderness, and aroma. Measure. Rinse. Add water. Close the lid. Press a button. You can walk away and know your rice cooker will care for the rest. It's like a friend who's got your back.

When cooking rice on the stovetop, there's more coddling and less time to walk away. You have to soak your rice for *x* amount of time. You need to bring it to a boil. Cover it. Simmer for *x* amount of time. Remove from the heat, but don't remove the lid. Fluff it. Let it rest again. After all that, the rice cooker's rice is just better. I mean, there is a reason why most homes in Hawai‘i have at least one rice cooker—sometimes more!

a guide to ingredients

This is a list of the ingredients that might prompt questions and, in turn, what I hope to be the answers you're looking for. It's not a list of every ingredient in the book, so if you don't see an ingredient listed, that's by design! I assume you know enough about all-purpose flour to pick the one you like.

BEANS

I will never ask you to do something I would not do, so I'm almost always calling for canned beans. The exception to this rule is when I'm making a beany soup without any meat. That bean broth is crucial, and I recommend using the best beans you can find. I always have a few bags of Rancho Gordo beans in my pantry.

BLACK LENTILS

All the lentil recipes in this book use black (beluga) lentils. I like Rancho Gordo's black caviar lentils, because I find their earthiness and ability to be tender yet hold their shape appealing.

BREADFRUIT (ʻULU)

This may be the first time you have heard about breadfruit, which is why I am so happy to share a bit about it. Breadfruit is a canoe crop, plants the Polynesian wayfinders brought with them to the islands in their canoes, and a staple food that grows on beautiful, expansive trees that can live up to a hundred years, maybe more. And it's said that one breadfruit tree can produce hundreds of pounds of fruit a year. The recipes in this book use mature breadfruit, which has a texture similar to a potato when cooked; think firm flesh. If you live outside of Hawaiʻi, the Hawaiʻi ʻUlu Cooperative's frozen precooked breadfruit wedges can be ordered online and shipped to the continental US.

FURIKAKE

This Japanese seasoning is made with dried seaweed, sesame seeds, salt, and sugar. I like Mishima brand's nori komi furikake.

GOCHUGARU

This is a Korean red chile flake with a gentle heat. If you can't find it, you can substitute Aleppo pepper.

GOCHUJANG

Also commonly spelled *kochujang* in Hawaiʻi, this is a spicy fermented Korean red chile paste. It can be found in most grocery stores in the Asian foods aisle.

GREEN ONION

Use both the green and white parts unless specified in the recipe. Also called scallions in parts of the US.

MISO

White (shiro) miso is my everyday miso and the only one I keep in my fridge. It's a sweetly delicate and mild miso that packs a lot of flavor without overpowering the dish.

MOCHIKO

Also called sweet rice flour and sometimes mochi flour, this is gluten-free. Koda Farms is my go-to.

NUTRITIONAL YEAST

It's inactive flakes of brewer's yeast, as in the same stuff used to make beer but deactivated and fortified with B_{12}. It has nutty, cheesy vibes and adds tons of umami to a dish.

OILS

Macadamia nut oil
This imparts a lot of nuttiness, and a little goes far.

Neutral oil
I like avocado or algae, but anything with a mild flavor, like corn, peanut, sunflower, or canola, will work.

Olive oil
I always call for extra-virgin olive oil.

Toasted sesame oil
Also called roasted sesame oil, this oil is very nutty and has a low smoke point. A little goes a long way.

VINEGARS

Cane vinegar

Made with, you guessed it, sugarcane! If you can't find it, you can substitute white vinegar, but note that it'll be a little more potent.

Rice vinegar

Look for plain old rice vinegar, not seasoned rice vinegar, which contains added sugars and salt. It's light and bright.

RICE

In this book, I call for Kokuho Rose rice, which is a medium-grain rice, in all recipes. It's an heirloom varietal from Koda Farms, but Calrose rice is a great substitute.

SALTS

ʻAlaea (Hawaiian salt)

This is a coarse sea salt and gained its name from the red alae volcanic clay that gives it that gorgeous brick-red color. You can substitute another coarse sea salt if you have trouble sourcing it.

Kosher salt

All recipes have been tested and written with Diamond Crystal kosher salt in mind. If you're using another brand of kosher salt, reduce the amount by about one-third.

SOY SAUCE (SHOYU)

Kikkoman is a good middle-of-the-road soy sauce. It's salty but not too salty. Adjust amounts accordingly if you're using a different brand. I like Aloha Shoyu for serving, as in drizzling a little on my eggs or on top of a finished dish.

STARCH

Potato starch vs. cornstarch

I find things turn out a little more tender when you're using potato starch, but if you can't find it or just prefer cornstarch, use cornstarch instead! Potato starch doesn't hold up well when cooking for long periods, so while you can substitute cornstarch for potato starch in most cases, you can't always substitute potato starch for cornstarch.

TARO (KALO)

Taro is a staple food in Hawaiʻi and one of the crops brought to the islands by Polynesian wayfinders, called a canoe crop or canoe plant. It must be cooked thoroughly to cook off the calcium oxalate, a chemical compound that can make you feel irritated and itchy. Generally, taro is a starchy root vegetable, sometimes compared to a potato. However, it's much more than that: It's firmer than a potato, stickier (in a good way), bouncier, nuttier, and usually sweeter. There's a wide range of taro, but in this book, I'm calling for the larger varieties commonly grown in Hawaiʻi. Today, there are about eighty native varieties and a broad range of leaf, stem, and corm colors within those varieties.

TARO LEAVES (LŪʻAU)

Taro leaves are the gorgeous, intensely green, heart-shaped leaves of a taro (kalo) plant. Just like taro, they must be cooked to be consumed. They, too, have calcium oxalate and can irritate. Taro leaves are most commonly used in laulau (pages 56 to 61) and lūʻau stews (pages 112 to 119). They have a mild, earthy flavor.

TOFU

There's a lot of tofu talk in this book. Most recipes call for firm tofu, which is typically found in the refrigerated section. When I call for silken tofu, I'm referring to the silken, soft tofu in the box in the Asian foods aisle (it's shelf-stable). When I call for soft tofu, the recipe uses the soft silken tofu from the refrigerated section. I hope this is helpful.

SWEET POTATO (ʻUALA)

A staple food and canoe crop, sweet potato is grown throughout the Hawaiian islands. Farmers (mahiʻai) developed many varieties throughout many generations, and today, there are around twenty-four different varieties of sweet potatoes grown in Hawaiʻi. Okinawan sweet potato, introduced by Okinawan and Japanese settlers, is one of the most common and popular types of sweet potato grown in Hawaiʻi today. With a light tan skin and fiercely purple flesh, I find it to be extra creamy and nutty compared to other sweet potato types. For this reason, all the recipes in this book use Okinawan sweet potatoes.

mains

The main dish is the center, which you plan your entire plate around. And while giving it that much weight might sound scary, it's the opposite for me. These dishes should spark joy and excitement for your next meal. You're likely already thinking about your main dish when building your plate. That's why this chapter sits at the front of the book. It's so that you can plan and build your menu. Each subchapter within this chapter represents a local Hawai'i dish or flavor rooted in a meaty protein, so think of the subchapters as flavor guides.

To use these "flavor guides," start by considering what you're craving. Say you're in the mood for a soup. Flip to the Bean Soup subchapter, and you'll find four soups to satisfy that craving. Or maybe you're in the mood for umami. Head to the Miso subchapter. Or pick something that reminds you of your favorite fried cutlet from the four Katsu variations. Once you've satisfied your "main" craving, head to the Starches and Sides chapters to see what speaks to you. In a creative rut? Head over to the Complete Meal Matrix at the back of the book (page 230) for ideas for what goes with what. Turn the page for a guide to the dishes that have inspired each subchapter. →

mains

SHOYU
A local Hawai'i mainstay, shoyu (soy sauce) chicken is chicken thighs braised in a sweet soy sauce infused with aromatics.

KATSU
Chicken, fish, or pork katsu is at its core a panko-crusted pan-fried protein that's either topped with katsu sauce or served with curry.

HULI HULI
Essentially a sweet local-style BBQ chicken, huli huli chicken is typically grilled and basted on a spit and "turn turn"-ed, which is what *huli huli* translates to.

MISO
Miso-braised pork is a pork butt or shoulder cooked low and slow in a sweet miso-soy sauce with ginger and garlic, until it becomes fall-apart tender.

LAULAU
Also written as lau lau, laulau is a traditional Hawaiian dish that is either baked or steamed. Most commonly made with pork, beef, or chicken and a piece of salted fish (like butterfish) wrapped in taro leaves (lūʻau) and ti or banana leaves.

BEAN SOUP
Portuguese bean soup is usually made with Portuguese sausage, kidney beans, cabbage, carrots, and potatoes. The broth is generally built with a ham hock, spices, and tomatoes.

LOCO MOCO
Comfort on a plate, loco moco is, in its essence, a burger set atop a bed of steamed white rice, loaded with brown gravy, and topped with a sunny-side up egg.

ADOBO
Filipino braised chicken and pork adobo are local Hawai'i food favorites. Cooked in a blend of vinegar, soy sauce (shoyu), garlic, black peppercorns, and bay leaves.

MOCHIKO
This is Hawai'i's version of fried chicken—marinated in a mixture of soy sauce, sweet rice flour (mochiko), cornstarch or potato starch, garlic, and eggs, this fried chicken is profoundly flavorful, lightly crisp, and a little chewy.

JUN
A uniquely Hawai'i dish, meat or fish jun is a local Hawai'i marinated version of the Korean dish soegogi-jeon, or beef jun. It's thinly sliced marinated meat that is dredged in flour and egg and pan-fried.

CHINESE-STYLE
In Hawai'i, if you say you're making something Chinese-style, it's reasonable to ask what kind of fish you're serving. That's because Chinese-style fish is a local favorite. It's a steamed fish finished with lots of aromatics and a hot oil.

LŪʻAU STEW
This is a Hawaiian dish that cooks down taro leaves (lūʻau) with coconut milk and is often made with squid or octopus (heʻe), chicken, or beef.

FURIKAKE
Furikake salmon is baked salmon brushed with mayonnaise and sprinkled with furikake, a Japanese seasoning. It is usually served with steamed white rice and roasted seasoned seaweed snacks.

Kāko'o 'Ōiwi, He'eia, 'Oahu

Shoyu Cauliflower with Chickpeas

It's absolutely acceptable to me if you judge a plate lunch spot based on its shoyu chicken. When I try out a new spot, I want each piece to be tender and flavored to the bone, with a good balance of sweet and salty. I thought about that when creating this recipe, as braising in a rich umami mixture lends itself well to vegetables, allowing them to soak up the flavorful liquid. Cauliflower takes some time to tenderize, making it perfect for this dish. Browning the wedges before braising adds a rich, caramelized flavor. Chickpeas added at the end beef up the dish and add a nice contrast to the texture of the cauliflower. This dish comes together quickly enough to make any night of the week.

Serves 4 to 6

1 large head cauliflower (2½ to 3 pounds)

3 tablespoons avocado oil

½ teaspoon kosher salt

½ red onion, diced

½ cup soy sauce (shoyu)

1 cup water

¼ cup packed light brown sugar

4 garlic cloves, finely grated

1½-inch piece fresh ginger, peeled and finely grated

Two 15-ounce cans chickpeas, drained and rinsed

2 tablespoons potato starch or cornstarch

4 green onions, green parts only, sliced on a bias

Trim the stem of the cauliflower so the head rests flush with the cutting board when placed stem-side down. Place the cauliflower on the board, stem-side down, and cut it in half through the core. Rest the halves, flat cut-side down, and cut each half through the core into thirds. You will have six wedges.

In a large, wide pan (with a lid), heat 1 tablespoon of the oil over medium-high heat until shimmering. Working in batches if necessary if your pan isn't big enough, add the wedges cut-side down, sprinkle with ¼ teaspoon of the salt, and cook until browned, about 3 minutes.

Add 1 tablespoon of the oil to the pan, flip the wedges over, sprinkle with the remaining ¼ teaspoon salt, and brown the other cut side. Set the browned wedges on a plate.

In the same pan, heat the remaining 1 tablespoon oil over medium heat until shimmering. Add the onion and sauté until it's just barely translucent, about 3 minutes.

Meanwhile, in a small bowl, whisk together the soy sauce, water, brown sugar, garlic, and ginger.

Return the wedges to the pan and pour the soy sauce mixture over them. Cover the pan, reduce the heat to medium-low, and simmer for 10 minutes. Flip the cauliflower wedges over and simmer for 10 more minutes with the lid on.

Uncover, increase the heat to medium, add the chickpeas, and cook for 2 minutes. While it's cooking, make a slurry by whisking 2 tablespoons cold water into the potato starch. Swirl the slurry into the pan and cook for another 2 minutes, or until it thickens. Remove from the heat. Toss in the green onions.

Serve immediately, spooning some of the braising liquid onto each portion.

Shoyu Kabocha with Green Onion Oil and Whipped Tofu

If you're new to kabocha, let me quickly sing its praises. It's a Japanese variety of winter squash that usually, although not always, has dark green skin; the skin is thin and can (and should) be eaten! Think of it as a soft, creamy, nutty, sweet, thin-skinned pumpkin. The shoyu (soy sauce) mixture imbues the kabocha with flavor while it cooks. Topped with a quick green onion oil and served over whipped tofu, this dish can be served warm, room temperature, or even chilled.

Serves 4

1 small kabocha (2 pounds)

½ cup soy sauce (shoyu)

1 cup water

¼ cup packed light brown sugar

4 garlic cloves, finely grated

1-inch piece fresh ginger, peeled and finely grated

Whipped Tofu (recipe follows)

Green Onion Oil (recipe follows)

Cut the kabocha in half first by removing the stem and making small cuts around the stem with the heel of your knife. Once you've made your way around the stem, do the same again, but use the tip of your knife to cut deeper. Repeat this process on the bottom of the squash. Use a rocking motion rather than trying to use brute force to cut the squash in half. Scoop the seeds out using a spoon. From here, cutting the squash into 2- to 2½-inch wedges should be easy; lean on the rocking motion versus using force to cut through. Cut those wedges into 2- to 2½-inch pieces. Try to make everything as uniform as possible, as it will help the squash cook more evenly. Set aside.

In a small bowl, whisk together the soy sauce, water, brown sugar, garlic, and ginger.

In your widest heavy-bottomed pot, arrange the kabocha pieces in an even single layer, skin-side down. Pour the soy sauce mixture over the kabocha and bring it to a boil over medium-high heat. Reduce the heat to medium-low, cover, and simmer until a knife pierces the middle of the squash with no resistance, 15 to 30 minutes. The cooking time will vary depending on the squash. Remove the pot from the heat and let the kabocha cool for at least 15 minutes and up to 30 minutes to allow it to absorb more liquid.

To serve, spoon the whipped tofu onto a plate, arrange the kabocha on top, and drizzle the green onion oil all over.

Whipped Tofu

Serves 4

One 12-ounce box soft silken tofu (shelf-stable, from the Asian foods aisle)

2 tablespoons fresh lemon juice

1 tablespoon white miso

1 teaspoon soy sauce (shoyu)

1 garlic clove, peeled but whole

½ teaspoon kosher salt

In a blender or food processor, combine the tofu, lemon juice, miso, soy sauce, garlic, and salt. Blend it on high for a minute or until smooth and creamy.

Green Onion Oil

Serves 4

2 tablespoons neutral oil (see page 18)

1-inch piece fresh ginger, peeled and julienned

2 garlic cloves, peeled and thinly sliced

2 green onions, chopped

¼ teaspoon kosher salt

In a small skillet, heat the oil over medium heat until shiny. Add the ginger, garlic, and green onions and sauté until the green onions are bright green and the garlic has softened, 1 to 2 minutes. Remove from the heat, sprinkle with the salt, and set aside.

Shoyu-Roasted Carrots with Butter Bean Puree

I have a thing for roasted carrots, as cooking them in a hot oven boosts their natural sweetness while tenderizing the inside and caramelizing the outside. It's a high-yield situation with low effort. Tossed in a quick shoyu sauce, these carrots are so good that you may find yourself doubling the batch. You'll find the temperature is lower here than what you might be accustomed to when roasting carrots. Roasting them a little longer at a lower temp makes that soy sauce (shoyu) sticky instead of burnt. Great as a main dish with the Butter Bean Puree, they are equally good served atop a Shaved Brussels Sprout and Cabbage Salad (page 170) or Ginger Cabbage Fried Farro (page 142).

Serves 4

Roasted Carrots and Garlic

2 pounds carrots, scrubbed

¼ cup soy sauce (shoyu)

2 tablespoons neutral oil (see page 18)

2 teaspoons light brown sugar

1 teaspoon honey

2 garlic cloves, finely grated

½-inch piece fresh ginger, peeled and finely grated

1 head garlic, top chopped off

1 tablespoon extra-virgin olive oil

¼ teaspoon kosher salt

Butter Bean Puree

2 teaspoons extra-virgin olive oil

¼ sweet onion, diced

1 teaspoon kosher salt

Two 15-ounce cans butter beans, drained and rinsed

½ cup vegetable broth

2 teaspoons white miso

1 teaspoon soy sauce (shoyu)

1 tablespoon fresh lemon juice

2 green onions, chopped

Roast the carrots and garlic: Preheat the oven to 400°F. Line a half-sheet pan with parchment paper.

Halve the carrots lengthwise, then cut into roughly 3-inch lengths. Place them in a large bowl and add the soy sauce, oil, brown sugar, honey, grated garlic, and ginger and give everything a good stir with either your hand or a wooden spoon. Pour the carrots onto the lined sheet pan and arrange into an even layer.

Set the head of garlic on a small piece of foil, pour the olive oil over the exposed cloves, and sprinkle with the salt. Wrap the foil tightly around the head of garlic. Nudge a couple of carrots over from the edge and place the head of garlic on the sheet pan.

Roast the carrots until they are tender and caramelized on the edges, about 40 minutes, flipping them halfway through. The garlic should be roasted in that time, too.

To make the butter bean puree: Start making the butter bean puree about 10 minutes before the carrots finish roasting. In a medium saucepan, heat the olive oil over medium heat until shiny. Add the onion and ½ teaspoon of the salt and sauté for 5 minutes. Add the beans, broth, miso, and remaining ½ teaspoon of salt and simmer briskly for 5 minutes. Remove the pan from the heat.

When the carrots are out of the oven, carefully unwrap the head of garlic and squeeze the cloves into the pan with the beans. Add the soy sauce and lemon juice and use an immersion blender to blend until super smooth. (Alternatively, you can transfer the contents to a food processor.)

To serve, spoon the bean puree onto a plate and top with the carrots and green onions. Serve immediately.

Shoyu Japanese Turnips with Oyster Mushrooms and Bok Choy

Japanese (aka Hakurei or Tokyo) turnips are white, thin-skinned, and sometimes called salad turnips. They are sweet and crisp, so much so that they can be eaten raw. I have friends who eat them like apples. Members of the brassica family, Japanese turnips require little more than a good scrub to prep. If you can't find Japanese turnips, look for other salad turnips, the most common one having gorgeous red skin. Avoid traditional American turnips with thick skins. This recipe uses the turnips two ways, first braising most of them until they're almost melty and then tossing diced chunks at the end for extra texture.

Serves 4

- ½ cup soy sauce (shoyu)
- 1 cup water
- ¼ cup packed light brown sugar
- 4 garlic cloves, peeled and finely grated
- Two 1-inch pieces peeled fresh ginger, one finely grated and the other finely julienned
- 2 pounds Japanese turnips, scrubbed
- 2 tablespoons extra-virgin olive oil
- ½ teaspoon kosher salt
- 2 tablespoons unsalted butter
- 8 ounces oyster mushrooms, cleaned and trimmed, torn into bite-size pieces
- 3 to 4 bunches baby bok choy (about 1 pound total), roughly chopped
- 3 green onions, chopped

In a small bowl, whisk together the soy sauce, water, brown sugar, garlic, and grated ginger. Set aside.

If your turnips came with greens, cut off the greens, leaving a short stem attached. Roughly chop the greens and set them aside. Halve each turnip from top to bottom; if the turnips are on the larger side, quarter them. Cut 2 or 3 of the whole turnips into ¼-inch dice and set aside.

In a large, wide pan (with a lid), heat 1 tablespoon of the olive oil over medium heat until shimmering. Add the turnip halves (or wedges) and sprinkle with ¼ teaspoon of the salt. Cook, tossing occasionally, until the turnips are golden on most of the cut sides, 3 to 4 minutes. Add the butter and remaining 1 tablespoon of olive oil and, when melted, add the mushrooms. Sprinkle with the remaining ¼ teaspoon salt and cook for 1 to 2 minutes, stirring often.

Pour in the soy sauce mixture. Cook, uncovered, for 10 minutes, stirring occasionally.

Reduce the heat to medium-low and add the bok choy and turnip greens (if you have them), gently stirring for a minute to combine. Cover with the lid and cook for 3 minutes untouched.

Uncover, add the reserved diced turnips, green onions, and julienned ginger, stir, and cook for about a minute. Serve immediately, spooning some of the braising liquid onto each portion.

Globe Eggplant Katsu

Chicken katsu is one of those dishes you can't help but picture when you think of plate lunch. A crisp pan-fried chicken cutlet drizzled with katsu sauce—it's a core memory for most. Eggplants are fantastic for this preparation because they can get tender and smoky simultaneously. I was inspired in part by tortang talong, a Filipino eggplant omelet made with a whole peeled and flattened eggplant. In Hawai'i, it's common to give it a healthy drizzle of soy sauce (shoyu) before digging in. It's one of the ultimate ways to eat eggplant because it is so tender and smoky, and it seamlessly melds with the egg, literally putting the egg in eggplant! It made sense to katsu it, using a globe eggplant instead of the typical Chinese or Japanese eggplant.

Serves 4

2 globe eggplants

Neutral oil (see page 18), for frying

¼ cup all-purpose flour

2 tablespoons potato starch

Kosher salt and freshly ground black pepper

2 large eggs, beaten

1 teaspoon soy sauce (shoyu)

1½ cups panko bread crumbs

Flaky salt, for serving

Katsu sauce (I like Bull-Dog Tonkatsu Sauce), for serving

Position an oven rack so it's in the top half, with enough room for the whole eggplant to sit on a quarter-sheet pan and not touch the heating element. Turn the broiler on high. Using a fork, prick both eggplants around 10 times each (this allows the steam to vent so the eggplant doesn't explode). Line a quarter-sheet pan with foil and arrange the eggplants on the sheet, ensuring they are not touching. Broil until they are charred on all sides, 20 to 25 minutes, rotating the eggplants a few times so they are evenly charred. Remove from the oven, wrap each eggplant in foil, and let sit for 10 minutes. Carefully peel off the charred skin, leaving the calyx and stem intact, and cut each eggplant in half, from stem to base.

Line a plate with paper towels and set it on the counter near the stove. In a large skillet, heat ¼ inch of oil over medium heat until it's shiny.

While the oil is heating, set up a dredging station in three shallow bowls: In the first bowl, combine the flour, potato starch, a pinch of salt, and a few cracks of pepper. In the second bowl, mix the eggs with the soy sauce. In the third bowl, add the panko. Dredge each eggplant half in the flour, shaking off any excess flour. Next, dip them into the eggs, allowing any excess to drip off before pressing them into the panko, coating both sides well. Place all the pieces on a plate and get ready to fry.

Working in batches, fry the eggplant in the hot oil until golden, 3 to 4 minutes on each side. Set on the paper towels to drain.

Serve immediately with a sprinkle of flaky salt and a drizzle of katsu sauce.

Potato Cake Katsu with Curry

One of the first dishes I learned how to make was Pommes Anna with my dad. Pommes Anna is a French potato "cake" made up of thinly sliced potatoes tossed in butter and salt that are layered in a pan, cooked first on the stovetop, and finished in the oven to produce a crispy outer crust and creamy interior. This katsu takes the basic concept of the Pommes Anna but gives it an earth-shatteringly crusty panko crust and marries it with a quick (box) curry. This is a plan-ahead katsu because the potato cake takes some time to bake and cool, but it's worth it for all those magical peel-apart layers!

Serves 4 to 6

Potato Cake

2 pounds Yukon Gold potatoes, peeled

3 tablespoons unsalted butter, melted

3 tablespoons extra-virgin olive oil

1½ teaspoons kosher salt

2 garlic cloves, finely grated

Curry

2 tablespoons neutral oil (see page 18)

½ sweet onion, diced

1 carrot, diced

1 celery stalk, diced

Kosher salt

1 garlic clove, finely grated

3 cups water

Half an 8.11-ounce box of House Foods Vermont Curry or half a 7.8-ounce box of S&B Golden Curry

Katsu

Neutral oil, for frying

¼ cup all-purpose flour

2 tablespoons potato starch

Kosher salt and freshly ground black pepper

2 large eggs, beaten

1¼ cups panko bread crumbs

½ cup finely grated Parmesan cheese

For Serving

Grated Parmesan cheese

1 green onion, thinly sliced

Cooked rice of your choice

To make the potato cake: Preheat the oven to 300°F. Line an 8 by 8-inch pan with parchment paper with excess on all sides to create "wings" that can be used to pull the cake out later. Set aside.

Using a mandoline or food processor with a slicing attachment, thinly slice (roughly ⅛ inch thick or thinner) the potatoes and place them in a large bowl. Toss with the melted butter, olive oil, salt, and garlic until evenly coated. Arrange the slices in the lined pan in an even layer, ensuring the edges of the potato slices overlap slightly to create a connected sheet of potato. Repeat layering until all the potatoes have been arranged in the pan. Bake for 2 hours or until golden on top and tender when pierced with a knife.

Set it on a rack to cool to room temperature, then cover the potato cake with a layer of parchment paper. Set another pan over the potato cake, fitting it in the potato cake pan, and fill that second pan with water or something heavy to weight it down. Transfer to the refrigerator for at least 2 hours and up to 24 hours to chill and compress.

When ready to make the katsu, make the curry: In a saucepan, heat the oil over medium heat until shiny. Add the onion, carrot, and celery, season with a pinch of salt, and sauté until the vegetables have softened, about 5 minutes. Add the garlic and sauté for a minute or until it's fragrant. Add the water and bring to a simmer. Reduce the heat to medium-low and simmer for 15 minutes.

Remove the pan from the heat and add the curry, stirring until dissolved. Return to low heat and cover the pan. When you're ready to serve, remove the lid and increase the heat to reduce the curry if you want it thicker.

To make the katsu: Lift the chilled, compressed potato cake from the pan and slide away from the parchment paper onto a cutting board. Cut the cake in half, then cut each half in thirds widthwise to create 6 bricks total.

Line a plate with paper towels and set it on the counter near the stove. In a large skillet, heat ¼ inch of oil over medium heat until it's shiny.

While the oil is heating, set up a dredging station in three shallow bowls: In the first bowl, combine the flour, potato starch, a pinch of salt, and a few cracks of pepper. In the second bowl, mix the eggs with a pinch of salt. In the third bowl, mix the panko with the Parmesan. Dredge each brick of potato cake in the flour, shaking off any excess flour. Next, dip them into the eggs, allowing any excess to drip off before pressing them into the panko mixture, coating both sides well. Place all the pieces on a plate and get ready to fry.

Working in batches, fry the potato cakes in the hot oil until golden, 3 to 4 minutes on each side. Set on the paper towels to drain.

Serve immediately with the curry, Parmesan, green onion, and rice.

Tofu Wasabi Pea Katsu

My friend Chelcy and her husband, Nick, are Maui couple goals; she's a phenomenal cook, and her husband is a hobbyist kayak-fisherman. Her fish katsu is the stuff of legend—her dad swears that her katsu is the best katsu he's ever had and her kids request it by name (they call it "crunchy fish"). And for good reason. There's nothing like a crunchy crust to take just about anything to the next level. There's a reason it's a local favorite. I'm hoping this tofu version, boosted by the pungent, earthy spice in the wasabi and my partner Moses's favorite pau hana (after-work) snack, wasabi peas, can live up to Chelcy's "crunchy fish." Wasabi peas are wasabi-coated roasted green peas that are perfectly spicy and go great with a beer In the afternoon. You can find them at local Hawai'i grocery stores or online.

Serves 4

One 16-ounce block firm tofu, drained

2 cups boiling water

Kosher salt

½ cup plus 2 tablespoons wasabi peas

Neutral oil (see page 18), for frying

¼ cup all-purpose flour

2 tablespoons potato starch

Freshly ground black pepper

2 large eggs, beaten

2 teaspoons wasabi paste

1 teaspoon soy sauce (shoyu)

1 cup panko bread crumbs

Katsu sauce (I like Bull-Dog Tonkatsu Sauce), for serving

Cut the tofu in half, crosswise, then flip the cut sides up and cut each piece in thirds so you end up with six rectangles. In a bowl, combine the boiling water, 2 tablespoons kosher salt, and the tofu. Let it sit for 10 minutes, then drain and pat the tofu dry with a clean kitchen towel or paper towels.

Meanwhile, in a food processor, pulse ½ cup of the wasabi peas until they resemble rice grains. Set aside. Crush the remaining 2 tablespoons wasabi peas (in a plastic bag if you want) on a cutting board using a jar to break them into smaller pieces. Reserve for serving.

Line a plate with paper towels and set it on the counter near the stove. In a large skillet, heat ¼ inch of oil over medium heat until it's shiny.

While the oil is heating, set up a dredging station in three shallow bowls: In the first bowl, combine the flour, potato starch, a pinch of salt, and a few cracks of pepper. In the second bowl, mix the eggs with the wasabi paste and soy sauce. In the third bowl, mix the panko with the ground wasabi peas. Dredge each slice of tofu in the flour, shaking off any excess flour. Next, dip them into the eggs, allowing any excess to drip off before pressing them into the panko, coating both sides well. Place all the pieces on a plate and get ready to fry.

Working in batches, fry the tofu in the hot oil until golden, 3 to 4 minutes on each side. Set on the paper towels to drain.

Serve immediately with a sprinkle of the reserved wasabi peas and a drizzle of katsu sauce.

Kohlrabi Steak Arare Katsu

This is a JUICY katsu. If you're new to kohlrabi, I think of it as a bulb of cabbage. This vegetable needs to be peeled to remove its tough and slightly bitter outer skin, but inside, it's mild yet sweet and super crunchy. Raw kohlrabi is great thinly sliced, added to salads, pickled, or even eaten like a chip with your favorite dip. But it transforms when cooked—it becomes succulent and juicy! I treat it like a steak and slice it thick so you have something substantial to cut into. The trick with this dish is to cook the kohlrabi until the edges turn translucent; you want it well cooked. The arare, a seasoned rice cracker that people here love to snack on, adds some extra dimension and flavor, but you can leave it out and sub more panko if you can't find it or don't want it! Be sure to serve this one with loads of quickles (pages 164 to 167) on the side.

Serves 4

Kosher salt

2 large kohlrabi, peeled and cut into ½-inch-thick rounds

½ cup plus 2 tablespoons arare

Neutral oil (see page 18), for frying

¼ cup all-purpose flour

2 tablespoons potato starch

Freshly ground black pepper

2 large eggs, beaten

1 teaspoon soy sauce (shoyu)

1 cup panko bread crumbs

Katsu sauce (I like Bull-Dog Tonkatsu Sauce), for serving

Line a plate with paper towels and have near the stove. Bring a large pot half filled with water to a boil over high heat and add 2 tablespoons salt. Add the kohlrabi, adding more water as needed to ensure they are fully submerged, and reduce the heat to medium. Cook until they are fork-tender with edges that are just translucent, 30 to 35 minutes. Set on the paper towels and gently run a fork over the top and bottom of each slice to form a light crosshatch pattern. This will help the flour to adhere to the steaks. Pat each steak dry.

Meanwhile, in a food processor, pulse ½ cup of the arare until it resembles rice grains. Set aside. Crush the remaining 2 tablespoons arare (in a plastic bag if you want) on a cutting board using a jar to break it into smaller pieces.

Line another plate with paper towels and set it on the counter near the stove. In a large skillet, heat ¼ inch of oil over medium heat until it's shiny.

While the oil is heating, set up a dredging station in three shallow bowls: In the first bowl, combine the flour, potato starch, a pinch of salt, and a few cracks of pepper. In the second bowl, mix the eggs with the soy sauce. In the third bowl, mix the panko with the processed arare. Dredge each kohlrabi steak in the flour, shaking off any excess flour. Next, dip them into the eggs, allowing any excess to drip off before pressing them into the panko, coating both sides well. Place all the pieces on a plate and get ready to fry.

Working in batches, fry the kohlrabi steaks in the hot oil until golden, 3 to 4 minutes on each side. Set on the paper towels to drain.

Serve immediately with a sprinkle of the reserved crushed arare and a drizzle of katsu sauce.

Bull-Dog
VEGETABLE & FRUIT SAUCE
(TONKATSU SAUCE)

Huli Huli Zucchini with Crispy Chickpeas

A few years ago, the internet was raving about Thomas Keller's zucchini roasting method, and for good reason: It can almost be described as transformative. The zucchini is pan-fried for 5 minutes, then transferred to a high-heat oven to roast, caramelizing and tenderizing the zucchini to perfection. I served this dish to a self-proclaimed zucchini hater, and she loved it! *Huli huli*, which translates to "turn turn," is used loosely here and points more toward the local style of barbecue sauce it's slathered in. It's typically made with chicken, grilled and basted in that delicious Hawai'i-style BBQ sauce and turn turn-ed while grilling and basting. Of course, you do turn the zucchini to coat it, so if you want to get technical . . . ;)

Serves 4

2 large zucchini

Kosher salt

Crispy Chickpeas

Two 15.5-ounce cans chickpeas, drained and rinsed

2 tablespoons potato starch

1 teaspoon garlic powder

1 teaspoon kosher salt

1 teaspoon ground sesame seeds

½ teaspoon freshly ground black pepper

3 tablespoons extra-virgin olive oil

½ teaspoon toasted sesame oil

Huli Huli Sauce

¼ cup ketchup

¼ cup soy sauce (shoyu)

¼ cup packed light brown sugar

2 tablespoons rice vinegar

½-inch piece fresh ginger, peeled and finely grated

1 garlic clove, finely grated

To Finish

2 tablespoons neutral oil (see page 18)

2 green onions, thinly sliced on a bias

Position racks in the top and bottom third of the oven and preheat the oven to 450°F. Line two half-sheet pans with parchment paper.

Cut the zucchini in half lengthwise and score the cut sides with a crosshatch pattern to create more surface for the salt to penetrate and later for the sauce to seep into. Sprinkle the cut sides with salt and let it sit for 10 minutes.

Meanwhile, prepare the crispy chickpeas: Place the chickpeas into a bowl and pat them dry with a clean kitchen towel or paper towels. Add the potato starch, garlic powder, salt, sesame seeds, and pepper and toss with your hands or a wooden spoon to coat them evenly. Drizzle on the olive oil and sesame oil and toss to coat again. Pour the chickpeas onto one of the lined sheet pans and roast on the upper rack for 20 to 25 minutes, until golden and crispy.

To make the huli huli sauce: In a bowl, whisk together the ketchup, soy sauce, brown sugar, vinegar, ginger, and grated garlic. Set aside.

To finish: In a large skillet, heat the neutral oil over medium-high heat until shiny. Pat the zucchini dry with paper towels, then place them cut-side down and cook untouched for 5 minutes.

Carefully transfer the zucchini to the remaining prepared sheet pan, cut-side down, and brush the huli huli sauce all over the skin side. Roast on the lower rack for 5 minutes. Flip the zucchini over, brush with more huli huli sauce, and roast for another 5 minutes cut-side up. (By now the chickpeas should be ready to come out of the oven.) Take the chickpeas out and turn on your broiler. Brush more sauce onto the cut side of the zucchini, put the zucchini on the upper rack, and broil on high for 1 to 2 minutes, until caramelized.

To serve, place the zucchini on a plate, cut-side up, sprinkle on the crispy chickpeas, and garnish with the green onions.

Huli Huli Tofu with Watercress

You'll never look back once you try any pan-fried glazed tofu, and this huli huli tofu is one of my favorite iterations. It's also one of the most requested meals in our house, our household of two, but still. My husband asked how I got the sauce to coat the tofu so well the first time I made it. Dredging the tofu in potato starch before frying does a couple of different things: It keeps the moisture in the tofu and creates a crispy crust that acts as the perfect surface for the sauce to cling to. The sweet and tangy huli huli sauce gives this dish an almost orange chicken kind of vibe. Mild and peppery watercress pairs perfectly and gives the dish a boost of freshness.

Serves 4

One 16-ounce block firm tofu, drained

2 cups boiling water

Kosher salt

¼ cup potato starch

Neutral oil (see page 18), for frying

Huli Huli Sauce

3 tablespoons ketchup

3 tablespoons soy sauce (shoyu)

3 tablespoons packed light brown sugar

1½ tablespoons rice vinegar

½-inch piece fresh ginger, peeled and finely grated

1 garlic clove, finely grated

Watercress

One 1-pound bunch watercress, ends trimmed, cut into 2-inch pieces

1 teaspoon distilled white vinegar

1 tablespoon neutral oil (see page 18)

2 garlic cloves, minced

¼-inch piece fresh ginger, peeled and minced

1 teaspoon soy sauce (shoyu)

½ teaspoon kosher salt

½ teaspoon granulated sugar

To Finish

2 green onions, thinly sliced on a bias

Cut the block of tofu in half lengthwise and then crosswise into ½-inch-thick squares.

In a bowl, combine the boiling water, 2 tablespoons salt, and the tofu. Let it sit for 10 minutes, then drain and pat the tofu dry with a clean kitchen towel or paper towels. Dry the bowl and add the potato starch to it.

Line a plate with paper towels and have near the stove. In a large skillet, heat 3 tablespoons of oil over medium heat until shiny.

Dredge the tofu pieces, one at a time, in the potato starch, then place them directly into the skillet. Working in batches, fry the tofu until golden brown and crispy on both sides, 3 to 5 minutes per side. Transfer the fried tofu to the paper towels. Add more oil as needed for the remaining batches. Wipe out any excess oil from the pan with a paper towel and reserve the pan.

To make the huli huli sauce: In a bowl, whisk together the ketchup, soy sauce, brown sugar, rice vinegar, ginger, and garlic. Set aside.

To prepare the watercress: Soak the watercress in a bowl of cold water with the white vinegar for 5 to 10 minutes. This ensures the watercress is as clean as possible and rehydrates the leaves. Drain and rinse thoroughly.

In the wiped-out skillet, heat the oil over medium-high heat until shiny. Add the garlic and ginger and sauté for 30 seconds or until fragrant. Add the watercress and cook for 2 to 3 minutes, stirring often. Drizzle on the soy sauce, sprinkle on the salt and sugar, and cook until the watercress is bright green and tender but not soggy, 1 to 2 minutes. Transfer to a plate to stop the cooking. Wipe out any excess moisture from the pan with a paper towel.

To finish: In the skillet, add the huli huli sauce to evenly coat the tofu. Set over medium heat and cook the sauce, stirring often, until the sauce has thickened, about 2 minutes. Return the tofu to the pan, flipping the pieces to ensure they're all coated in sauce.

Serve with the watercress and top with the green onions.

Huli Huli Cauliflower Steaks with Cauliflower Puree

The problem with cauliflower steaks is that you only get a few steaks out of every cauliflower and are left with loads of broken pieces. This dish uses those broken bits to make a beautiful puree to serve with your gorgeous cauliflower steaks. The creamy puree is sneakily loaded with extra protein from the cannellini beans, making this dish a little heartier than it might look.

Serves 4 to 6

2 large heads cauliflower

6 tablespoons extra-virgin olive oil

Kosher salt and freshly ground black pepper

Huli Huli Sauce

¼ cup ketchup

¼ cup soy sauce (shoyu)

¼ cup packed light brown sugar

2 tablespoons rice vinegar

½-inch piece fresh ginger, peeled and finely grated

1 garlic clove, finely grated

Cauliflower Puree

1 tablespoon unsalted butter

1 tablespoon extra-virgin olive oil

½ sweet onion, diced

2 garlic cloves, minced

¼ cup heavy cream

¼ cup vegetable broth

Half a 15-ounce can cannellini beans, drained and rinsed

2 sprigs cilantro, coarsely chopped, for serving

Position racks in the top and bottom thirds of the oven and preheat the oven to 450°F.

To cut the cauliflower into steaks, remove any outer leaves and trim the stem so that it is close to the head of the cauliflower. This gives it a good base for cutting the steaks. Cut one of the heads of cauliflower in half through the core, then cut each half into ¾-inch steaks. You should have 4 to 6 steaks. Reserve the pieces that break off. Repeat for the second head of cauliflower. Set the steaks on a half sheet pan, evenly spacing them to ensure none are touching. Drizzle the steaks with 3 tablespoons of the olive oil and lightly season with salt and pepper. Break down any larger pieces of the reserved cauliflower into pieces that are roughly the same size. Arrange them on a second half sheet pan and drizzle with the remaining 3 tablespoons olive oil and salt and pepper to taste.

Transfer both sheets to the oven and roast until golden brown and caramelized around the edges, 30 to 35 minutes, rotating the pans from top to bottom halfway through roasting.

Meanwhile, to make the huli huli sauce: In a bowl, whisk together the ketchup, soy sauce, brown sugar, vinegar, ginger, and garlic. Set aside.

Start the cauliflower puree: Halfway through the roasting, get started on the puree. In a medium saucepan, combine the butter and olive oil and heat over medium heat until the butter has melted. Add the onion and garlic and sauté until softened, 3 to 4 minutes. Add the heavy cream, vegetable broth, and beans and simmer for 5 minutes.

When the cauliflower is done roasting, set the pan with the cauliflower steaks aside and add the cauliflower pieces to the saucepan. Simmer for 5 minutes, then carefully transfer the contents of the saucepan to a high-powered blender and blend until smooth. (Alternatively, you can use an immersion blender.)

Turn the oven to broil and brush both sides of the cauliflower steaks generously with the sauce, then broil until the sauce begins to caramelize, 2 to 3 minutes. Watch closely, as it can go from caramelized to burnt very quickly.

Serve atop the cauliflower puree and sprinkle with the chopped cilantro.

Huli Huli Hasselback Butternut Squash

I remember seeing a Hasselback butternut squash in an old *Bon Appétit* magazine and thinking, "Wow, that is the fanciest squash I've ever seen." Well, it turns out that it's not that hard to achieve as long as you've got a couple of chopsticks and a decent knife. It transforms an ordinary butternut squash into something extraordinary because it increases the surface area exponentially, allowing you to infuse it with huli huli sauce.

Serves 4

One 3-pound butternut squash

1 tablespoon extra-virgin olive oil

¼ cup ketchup

¼ cup soy sauce (shoyu)

¼ cup packed light brown sugar

2 tablespoons rice vinegar

½-inch piece fresh ginger, peeled and finely grated

1 garlic clove, finely grated

1 green onion, thinly sliced, for garnish

Preheat the oven to 425°F. Line a half-sheet pan with parchment paper.

Peel the butternut squash and use a rocking motion rather than trying to use brute force to cut the squash in half lengthwise. Scoop the seeds out using a spoon. Place both halves, cut-side down, on the lined sheet pan, brush the cut squash on all sides with the olive oil, and roast for 15 minutes to soften the squash.

While the squash is roasting, in a bowl, whisk together the ketchup, soy sauce, brown sugar, vinegar, ginger, and garlic to make the huli huli sauce. Set aside.

Remove the sheet pan from the oven and let the squash sit on the pan until it's cool enough to touch. Move one half to a cutting board and set it with a long side facing you. Place two chopsticks on either side, the long way. The chopsticks act as a guard to stop you from cutting all the way through the squash. Cut thin crosswise slits along the length of the squash until you hit or almost just hit the chopsticks. Carefully move the Hasselbacked half back to the sheet pan and repeat the process with the other half. Brush the squash halves with the huli huli sauce, brushing as much sauce between the slices as possible.

Return to the oven and roast for 1 hour or until tender and deeply caramelized, brushing on more sauce every 15 minutes.

Serve immediately. Garnish with the green onion.

Miso Cabbage with Oyster Mushrooms

I usually make a miso pork roast when I know I have semi-picky eaters coming for dinner. As my husband, Moses, says, "Who doesn't love salty, sweet meat?" I remember a dinner a few years ago when my godchildren (and their parents) were coming for a celebratory sushi dinner. I knew my goddaughter wasn't a wildly ambitious eater at the time, so I made a pot of miso pork for her. One by one I noticed everyone else getting up from the table to help themselves to some pork and rice casually, and by the end of the meal, we had sushi left over because the pork was such a hit. This cabbage is reminiscent of miso pork, tender and almost falling apart; the mushrooms add some meatiness, and the onions melt in your mouth.

Serves 4

1 large head green cabbage

3 tablespoons mayonnaise

2 tablespoons neutral oil (see page 18), plus more as needed

2 tablespoons unsalted butter

1 sweet onion, thinly sliced

6 ounces oyster mushrooms, torn into bite-size pieces

3 tablespoons white miso

3 tablespoons soy sauce (shoyu)

2 tablespoons sugar

½ cup water

3 garlic cloves, finely grated

½-inch piece fresh ginger, peeled and finely grated

1 green onion, chopped, for serving

Preheat the oven to 400°F.

Cut off the tough stem at the end of the cabbage, avoiding cutting through any leaves. Cut the head through the core into 6 to 8 wedges, keeping the core attached to each wedge; this keeps them intact when cooking. Brush all cut sides with the mayonnaise.

In your widest Dutch oven, heat the oil over medium-high heat until shiny. Add half the cabbage wedges, cut-side down, and sear until browned on both cut sides, 3 to 4 minutes per side. Set the cabbage aside on a plate and repeat with the second batch, adding more oil to the pan as necessary. Set the second batch on the plate.

Melt the butter in the pan over medium heat, then add the onion and mushrooms. Sauté until the onion has softened and the mushrooms have some color, 6 to 8 minutes.

Meanwhile, in a small bowl, whisk together the miso, soy sauce, sugar, water, garlic, and ginger.

Return the cabbage wedges to the pan, nudging some onion and mushrooms aside to arrange the wedges in an even layer. Pour the miso sauce over the cabbage. Remove from the heat, cover, and transfer to the oven to roast for 30 minutes. Remove the lid and roast for another 15 minutes or until the liquid has reduced a bit.

Serve immediately with the green onion on top.

Miso Beets with Cannellini Beans

I tend to default to roasting beets because that's the first way I learned to cook them. However, one day, I was talking to my friend Jackie, and she said she usually boils hers. Forgive me for my ignorance, but my gut response was, "What? You boil them?" As it turns out, this is a perfectly normal and maybe the number one way to prepare beets. And it yields something so soft and tender, enhancing their natural sweetness, that I wonder how I didn't boil them sooner! This recipe leans on tender, sweet boiled beets, coating them in a silky miso sauce with creamy cannellini beans and savory green onions. This dish is great served with steamed white rice and some everyday quickles (see page 164).

Serves 4

2 pounds golden beets, scrubbed and trimmed

2 tablespoons unsalted butter

½ cup water

2 tablespoons white miso

2 tablespoons soy sauce (shoyu)

1 tablespoon sugar

2 garlic cloves, finely grated

¼-inch piece fresh ginger, peeled and finely grated

½ teaspoon kosher salt

One 15-ounce can cannellini beans, drained and rinsed

3 green onions, cut into 1-inch lengths

Cooked rice of your choice, for serving

Set up a large bowl of ice and water and have near the stove. In a large pot, combine the beets with water to cover by 1 inch and bring to a boil. Boil the beets until you can easily pierce them with a fork, 20 to 40 minutes. The range is wide because it depends on the size of the beets. Immediately transfer the boiled beets to the ice bath.

When cool enough to touch, peel the beets with your hands; the skins should slide off easily. You can wear gloves if you're worried about the beets staining your hands and nails. Slice the beets into 1-inch-thick rounds.

In a large, wide Dutch oven, melt the butter over medium heat. Stir in the water, miso, soy sauce, sugar, garlic, ginger, and salt. Nestle in the beet rounds and add the beans and green onions. Reduce the heat to medium-low and cook, flipping the beets at least once, until the sauce has thickened slightly, 5 to 7 minutes.

Serve immediately with the rice of your choice, spooning some of the sauce onto a bowl or plate.

Roasted Miso Sweet Potato with Pumpkin Seeds

The secret to these potatoes is covering and then roasting them with enough liquid to add some moisture to the flesh of the potato while infusing them with flavor at the same time. They're a little melty and a little moist. The first time my friend Lily saw them, her reaction was "Yum!" This one's for the sweet potato lovers.

Serves 4

2 pounds Okinawan sweet potatoes ('uala), scrubbed

1 cup water

2 tablespoons white miso

2 tablespoons soy sauce (shoyu)

2 tablespoons unsalted butter, melted

1 tablespoon sugar

2 garlic cloves, finely grated

¼-inch piece fresh ginger, peeled and finely grated

½ cup pumpkin seeds

2 tablespoons neutral oil (see page 18)

3 green onions, chopped

Kosher salt

Preheat the oven to 425°F.

Cut the sweet potato into 1½-inch pieces; they need not be uniform. In a large bowl, whisk together the water, miso, soy sauce, butter, sugar, garlic, and ginger. Add the sweet potatoes and toss to evenly coat. Pour everything into your widest Dutch oven and arrange it in an even layer. Cover with the lid or foil if you don't have a lid.

Transfer to the oven and roast for 30 minutes.

When you take it out, vent the lid slightly and let the sweet potatoes rest in the pan.

Meanwhile, in a small saucepan, toast the pumpkin seeds over medium heat, shaking the pan to move them around, until golden brown, 3 to 5 minutes. Set aside on a plate.

Add the oil to the pan and heat over medium heat until shiny. Add the green onions and cook for a minute or two, using a spatula to stir a few times, until the green onions are bright and wilted. Remove from the heat, sprinkle with a pinch of salt, and return the pumpkin seeds to the pan. Give everything a quick stir.

Plate the sweet potato and top with the pumpkin seeds, serving immediately.

Braised Miso Eggplant

Sometimes, eggplant gets a bad rap unnecessarily. It's true it can become a soggy mess if you're not careful, so it's all about knowing how to cook it. This recipe takes a few steps to prevent that by seasoning it with salt to draw out some of the bitterness and moisture. The second step is to lightly coat it in cornstarch before frying it. This gives the eggplant a bit of a barrier, preventing it from soaking up too much oil, which leads to sogginess. After that, it's braised in the miso sauce for a short time, yielding a delicately tender eggplant dish that will impress even the most skeptical eggplant eaters.

Serves 2

1 pound Japanese or Chinese eggplant (roughly 2 large eggplants)

2 teaspoons kosher salt

2 tablespoons white miso

2 tablespoons soy sauce (shoyu)

1 tablespoon sugar

½ cup water

3 tablespoons neutral oil (see page 18)

4 teaspoons cornstarch

2 garlic cloves, minced

¼-inch piece fresh ginger, peeled and minced

2 green onions, sliced on a bias, for serving

2 lime wedges, for serving

Trim the calyx and stems (carefully if they have spines) from the eggplants before slicing on a bias into ½-inch-thick disks. Place the pieces in a colander set in a bowl or the sink and toss with the salt. Let it sit for 15 minutes before rinsing off the salt. Pat the eggplant pieces dry with a clean kitchen towel and lay them on the towel to dry thoroughly before cooking. You want the eggplant to be as dry as possible.

In a small bowl, whisk together the miso, soy sauce, sugar, and water. Set aside.

Line a plate with paper towels and have near the stove. In a large skillet, heat 2½ tablespoons of the oil over medium-high heat until shiny. Toss the eggplant with the cornstarch to coat it evenly, then immediately add it to the skillet, arranging it so none of the pieces touch. Reduce the heat to medium and cook until each side is golden brown, 4 to 5 minutes per side. Transfer to the paper towels.

Return the skillet to medium heat, and heat the remaining ½ tablespoon oil until shiny. Add the garlic and ginger and sauté for 30 seconds. Remove the skillet from the heat and pour in the sauce. Return the eggplant to the skillet and set it over medium-low heat. Stir until the eggplant is well coated in the sauce and thickens slightly. Garnish with the green onions and serve immediately with lime wedges.

Laulau

Opening a laulau (also written *lau lau*) feels like unwrapping a present, as each one is a package or a bundle that looks like a gift. It's a traditional Hawaiian food usually comprising a protein like pork seasoned with ʻalaea (Hawaiian red salt) and a piece of salted fish wrapped in lūʻau (taro leaves). That parcel is then wrapped in ti leaves and cooked. Traditionally, it's cooked in an imu (underground oven or pit) over hot rocks, though now it's common to steam them on the stovetop or in a pressure cooker or bake them in the oven. Vegetable-packed laulau isn't the standard, but more and more veggie versions are popping up! When choosing your veggies, look for heartier ones that hold up well when cooked for an extended period. While miso and shoyu aren't traditional flavors for a laulau, I find they work beautifully. My partner Moses's mom, who is no stranger to making laulau—in fact, I think of her as the laulau queen—was blown away by how tasty the veggies in these laulau are. She told me she'll be making more veggie laulau in the future, which is the ultimate compliment. I've broken the recipe up into six simple steps for making your custom veggie laulau.

Makes 6 laulau

Step One: Prep the Leaves

18 taro leaves (lūʻau), about 1½ pounds

6 large ti leaves

Taro leaves: Put on some gloves if your skin is sensitive. Wash the leaves well and pat dry. With a paring knife, remove the thick center stem and tough veins, keeping the leaf intact.

Ti leaves: Wash the ti leaves and pat dry. Strip off the stiff midrib of the leaf by cutting a small notch about midway down the leaf and using your hands to gently remove the rib while keeping the leaf intact.

Substitutions: You can substitute collard greens or Swiss chard for the taro leaves. Prep the leaves as above but blanch the greens to soften before proceeding to the next step.

Banana leaves can be used in place of ti leaves. Cut a few banana leaves into 6 by 14-inch pieces.

continued →

Step Two: Choose the Filling(s)

While I've pulled together four combinations that work really well, you can mix and match the fillings according to what you like most or what you have on hand. Just stick with hearty veggies that hold up to long cook times. I've had great success with sweet potato, carrots, taro (kalo), breadfruit ('ulu), kabocha squash, Japanese (Tokyo/Hakurei) turnips, daikon, beet, and oyster mushrooms. Additionally, you can add sliced sweet onions, thinly sliced garlic, and/or thinly sliced peeled fresh ginger to any bundle.

Four Tasty Combos

Sweet Potato, Mushroom, Onion, and Garlic Laulau
1 pound Okinawan sweet potato ('uala), peeled and cut into 1½-inch pieces + 1½ oyster or king trumpet mushrooms, torn into bite-size pieces + thinly sliced sweet onion + 3 cloves thinly sliced garlic

Breadfruit, Kabocha, and Ginger Laulau
1 pound breadfruit ('ulu), peeled and cut into 1½-inch pieces + 1 pound kabocha squash, cut into 1½-inch pieces + 1-inch piece thinly sliced peeled fresh ginger

Carrot, Turnip, Beet, Onion, Garlic, and Ginger Laulau
8 ounces carrots, scrubbed and cut into 1½-inch pieces + 8 ounces turnips, trimmed and cut into 1½-inch pieces + 1 pound beets, peeled and cut into 1½-inch pieces + thinly sliced sweet onion + 3 cloves thinly sliced garlic + 1-inch piece thinly sliced peeled fresh ginger

Taro, Sweet Potato, Daikon, and Garlic Laulau
1 pound taro (kalo) + 8 ounces Okinawan sweet potato ('uala), peeled and cut into 1½-inch pieces + 8 ounces daikon, cut into 1½-inch pieces + 3 cloves thinly sliced garlic

Step Three: Season the Filling

There are a few options when it comes to seasoning your laulau. Traditionally, laulau are seasoned with 'alaea (Hawaiian red salt). The miso and shoyu options are easy to prepare and add an extra depth of flavor.

For the Purist:

'Alaea (Hawaiian red salt)

Toss your veggies of choice in a bowl with a few big pinches of 'alaea.

Make It Miso:

1 tablespoon miso

1 tablespoon soy sauce (shoyu)

1 tablespoon water

1 teaspoon sugar

2 garlic cloves, finely grated

⅛-inch piece fresh ginger, peeled and finely grated

In a large bowl, whisk together the miso, soy sauce, water, sugar, garlic, and ginger. Toss your choice of veggies in the mixture.

Make It Shoyu:

1 tablespoon neutral oil (see page 18)

2 tablespoons soy sauce (shoyu)

1 tablespoon maple syrup

1 garlic clove, finely grated

⅛-inch piece fresh ginger, peeled and finely grated

In a large bowl, whisk together the oil, soy sauce, maple syrup, garlic, and ginger. Toss your choice of veggies in the mixture.

Laulau, continued

Step Four: Assemble

The secret to a good laulau is fat. There's no way around it. Nobody wants to cut into the perfectly tender taro leaves only to find dry meat in the center. The same goes for veggies. You need to add fat; I find butter the best for mouthfeel and richness.

3 to 6 tablespoons unsalted butter, cut into ½-tablespoon pieces

Assemble the parcels by stacking 3 taro leaves, vein-side down, with the largest leaf on the bottom and the smallest leaf on top. Add a sixth of your veggies (in most cases, this is roughly the size of a baseball) in the middle. Add ½ to 1 tablespoon of butter to each bundle. Fold in the left and right sides tightly, then fold the bottom up tightly before folding the top over and rolling tightly until the parcel is closed. Repeat this until all parcels have been rolled.

To wrap the parcels, set a ti leaf down. Place the parcel seam-side down a few inches below the top tip of the leaf and fold the ti leaf over the bundle, continuing to fold and roll until the bundle is securely wrapped in the ti leaf. Split the stem in half and use to tie each bundle shut or use some kitchen string to tie it closed. Repeat until all 6 have been wrapped.

continued →

Laulau, continued

Step Five: Cook

There are three ways you can cook the laulau. They are all steaming through different methods: stovetop, pressure cooker, and oven.

Stovetop

Set a steamer basket over a large pot or pan filled with water to a height of 3 to 4 inches. Bring the water to a boil over medium-high heat, then promptly reduce the heat to medium-low to keep at a steady simmer. Set the laulau in the basket and replace the lid. Steam for 4 hours; check the water level as you steam and replenish it as needed. Set the laulau on a plate to rest for at least 10 minutes. If you're using collard greens, the cooking time is the same. For Swiss chard, reduce the cooking time by 1 hour.

Pressure Cooker

Place the trivet on the bottom of your pressure cooker and add 2 cups water. Place the laulau on the trivet in the cooker, close the lid, and cook on high pressure for 1 hour 10 minutes with at least 15 minutes of natural pressure release. Set the laulau on a plate to rest for at least 10 minutes. If you're using collard greens, the cooking time is the same. For Swiss chard, reduce the cooking time by 20 minutes.

Oven

Preheat the oven to 350°F. Set a wire rack in a roasting pan and pour in ½ inch or so of water. As long as the bottom of the rack doesn't touch the water, you're fine. Place the laulau on the rack, then cover the pan with foil, ensuring it's tightly sealed around the edges to keep the steam in. Roast for 4 hours 30 minutes. Set the laulau on a plate to rest for at least 10 minutes. If you're using collard greens, the cooking time is the same. For Swiss chard, reduce the cooking time by 45 minutes.

Step Six: Serve

Carefully remove the outer ti leaves, discarding them as they are not edible. Optionally top with Green Onion Oil (page 27) and Coconut Cream (below).

Coconut Cream: This thickened coconut cream is inspired by a beautiful vegan restaurant called ʻAi Love Nalo in Waimanalo on the island of Oʻahu, run by my Aunty Malia Smith (not by blood) and her daughter. They serve a laulau that they top with a coconut cream.

Add a 13.5-ounce can of coconut cream to a saucepan and set it over medium heat. Cook until it simmers, then make a slurry by whisking 1 tablespoon cornstarch with 1 tablespoon cold water. Remove the pan from the heat and stream the slurry into the cream, whisking continuously. Return the pan to the heat and cook, stirring frequently, until the mixture has thickened, 2 to 3 minutes.

Kākoʻo ʻŌiwi

Location
Heʻeia, Oʻahu, Hawaiʻi

Farm Stats
405 acres, currently farming 26 acres
25-foot elevation

Growing
Kalo (taro), maiʻa (banana), ʻulu (breadfruit), kō (sugarcane)

Established
2006

Owners
Community-based nonprofit organization

Kākoʻo ʻŌiwi is a farm that's committed to providing sustainably farmed fresh produce for local communities, creating a place and space for the community to develop and nurture a meaningful cultural connection with the ʻāina (land). Their mission is not only to create access to locally grown and fresh produce but also to educate and engage the people of Hawaiʻi.

The team at Kākoʻo ʻŌiwi devote their energies to restoring the cultural connection between the people and the land. There's a lot of community involvement on the farm, from community workdays to mālama ʻāina (care for and honor the land) to weekly offerings of poi (a traditional Hawaiian dish made from cooked and pounded corms of kalo/taro), kūlolo (a Hawaiian dessert made from kalo/taro, coconut milk, and sugar), and steamed lūʻau (taro leaves) to make it easier for locals to incorporate locally grown foods into their lives. The farm is viewed as a place where families can gather for celebration, learning, and healing. When you're there, it's easy to imagine all the farm will become, but it's also comforting to know that the land will be preserved for future generations.

When writing *Aloha Kitchen*, I asked a friend at Kākoʻo ʻŌiwi if they had any pohole fern since I was developing a recipe for a pohole fern salad. He said, "Stop by, no problem, we've got lots." When I say it was the prettiest, healthiest pohole I've seen, I'm not exaggerating. When my husband, Moses, and I pulled up to the farm, I was taken aback by how green it was and honestly didn't realize how big it would be. And that was more than six years ago. Today, the team has restored over six acres of loʻi kalo (irrigated terraces for taro production) and twenty acres for māla (dryland) diversified agriculture.

Hearty Veggie Portuguese Bean Soup

Serves 6

Shiitake Broth

3 dried shiitake mushrooms, rinsed and cleaned to remove debris

3 cups hot water

Soup

1 tablespoon unsalted butter

1 to 2 tablespoons extra-virgin olive oil

1 sweet onion, diced

2 teaspoons kosher salt, plus more as needed

2 carrots, roughly chopped

2 celery stalks, roughly chopped

2 Yukon Gold potatoes, peeled and cut into 1-inch cubes

2 garlic cloves, finely grated

1 tablespoon Better Than Bouillon vegetable base

One 14.5-ounce can diced tomatoes

One 8-ounce can tomato sauce

1 tablespoon ketchup

1 tablespoon soy sauce (shoyu)

1 bay leaf

¼ teaspoon ground cinnamon

Ground cloves

½ teaspoon smoked paprika

1 teaspoon freshly ground black pepper

3 cups Soup Beans (recipe follows), made with kidney beans or red beans

1 to 1½ cups bean cooking broth

1 small head cabbage, cored and cut into bite-size pieces

1 cup coarsely chopped fresh cilantro

Lemon wedges, for serving

Whenever a rainy day hits, all I want is Portuguese bean soup, a dish introduced to the islands by the Portuguese. Almost every family has their take on it, but for me, the warming spices are crucial. Typically, it's all about the broth that comes from cooking a smoked ham hock or shank low and slow. For this veggie-packed (read: meat-free) version, cooking your beans versus using canned beans is the secret to building a rich and flavorful soup: The magic is in the bean broth. I learned how to cook a proper pot of beans from my favorite source of beans, Rancho Gordo, and their method heavily inspired this bean recipe. The broth created when you soak dried shiitake mushrooms and add a dash of shoyu and a pinch of smoked paprika brings forth notes of umami and smoke reminiscent of this soup's meatier predecessor. The touch of butter provides a satiny mouthfeel. Don't skip the lemon wedges at the end; they add brightness and boost all the flavors in this soup!

To make the shiitake broth: In a bowl, combine the shiitakes and the hot water and soak for 20 minutes. Scoop out the shiitakes and squeeze the excess liquid back into the bowl. Save the shiitakes for another use. Set the shiitake broth aside.

To make the soup: In a large pot, combine the butter and 1 tablespoon of the olive oil and heat over medium heat until shiny. Add the onion and ½ teaspoon of the salt and sauté until the onion is just translucent and fragrant, about 5 minutes.

Add the carrots and celery with another ½ teaspoon of the salt and cook for 3 minutes, stirring occasionally, then add the remaining 1 tablespoon olive oil if needed. Add the potatoes and ½ teaspoon of the salt and cook for 5 minutes, stirring a few times. Add the garlic and cook for 30 seconds before adding 2 cups of the shiitake broth, bouillon base, diced tomatoes, tomato sauce, ketchup, soy sauce, bay leaf, cinnamon, a small pinch of cloves, the smoked paprika, pepper, and the remaining ½ teaspoon salt. Stir to combine, then increase the heat to medium-high to bring to a boil.

Reduce the heat to medium-low, cover, and simmer until the vegetables are tender, 40 to 50 minutes. Taste the soup and adjust the salt to taste.

Add the beans, 1 to 1½ cups of the reserved bean broth, the remaining 1 cup of shiitake broth to top up the liquid, if needed, and the cabbage and cook for 15 more minutes. Add the cilantro and cook for 5 more minutes.

Ladle the soup into bowls and serve with lemon wedges. Store any leftovers in an airtight container in the refrigerator for up to 3 days.

Soup Beans

Makes 3 cups

- 1 tablespoon extra-virgin olive oil
- ½ sweet onion, diced
- 2 garlic cloves, smashed and peeled
- 8 ounces (about 1¼ cups) dried kidney or red beans, soaked for 2 to 6 hours, then drained
- 6 cups water
- 1½ to 2 teaspoons kosher salt

In a large pot, heat the olive oil over medium heat. Add the onion and garlic and sauté until the onion is just translucent and fragrant, about 5 minutes. Add the beans and water and bring to a rapid boil over medium-high heat. Boil the beans for 15 minutes, reducing the heat if boiling too vigorously. Reduce the heat to medium-low and partially cover the pot with a lid. Simmer the beans until they are tender, 1 to 3 hours, depending on the beans you're using.

When the beans are soft enough that you can bite through them easily, add the salt to taste. You may need to add more water during cooking. If preparing the beans beforehand, let them cool to room temperature before transferring them in their broth to the fridge in an airtight container.

Shiitake and Bok Choy with Chickpea Soup

On the surface, this soup looks nothing like Hearty Veggie Portuguese Bean Soup (page 64), but if you look at the soups' general formulas, they follow the same basic ratios and recipe structure. Replacing the diced tomatoes and tomato sauce with more shiitake broth takes this soup in a new direction. Adding white miso and baby bok choy leans into familiar flavors while creating something different. I love that soups have infinite possibilities once you master the ratios and methods for building flavor. The bok choy is added both during the cooking process and at the end as a topping, allowing you to enjoy layers of flavor. The chickpeas add some nice variation in texture and a nuttiness that pairs beautifully with the heat of the ginger.

Serves 6

Shiitake Broth

12 dried shiitake mushrooms, rinsed and cleaned to remove debris

6 cups hot water

Soup

8 baby bok choy (2 pounds total)

1 tablespoon unsalted butter

2 tablespoons extra-virgin olive oil

1 sweet onion, diced

2 teaspoons kosher salt, plus more as needed

4 garlic cloves, thinly sliced

1 tablespoon Better Than Bouillon vegetable base

2-inch piece fresh ginger, peeled and finely julienned

2 tablespoons white miso

1 tablespoon soy sauce (shoyu)

1 teaspoon freshly ground black pepper

3 cups Soup Beans (page 65), made with chickpeas

1 to 1½ cups chickpea cooking broth, to taste

1 cup coarsely chopped fresh cilantro

To make the shiitake broth: In a bowl, combine the shiitakes and the hot water and soak for 20 minutes. Scoop out the shiitakes and squeeze the excess liquid back into the bowl. Cut off any tough stems and thinly slice the shiitake mushroom caps, then add them to the shiitake broth and set aside.

To make the soup: Chop 5 of the baby bok choy into bite-size pieces, and discard the stems, and set aside. Cut the remaining 3 bok choy in half (or quarters if they're a little large) lengthwise, through the stem, and set aside.

In a large pot, combine the butter and 1 tablespoon of the olive oil and heat over medium heat until shiny. Add the onion and ½ teaspoon of the salt and sauté until the onion is just translucent and fragrant, about 5 minutes.

Add the garlic and cook for 1 to 2 minutes, then add the shiitake broth with the sliced shiitakes, bouillon base, chopped bok choy, ginger, miso, soy sauce, pepper, and the remaining 1½ teaspoons salt. Stir to combine, then increase the heat to medium-high to bring to a boil. Reduce the heat to medium-low, cover, and simmer for 30 minutes. Taste the soup and adjust the salt to taste.

Add the chickpeas and chickpea broth and cook for 15 more minutes.

Meanwhile, in a medium skillet, heat the remaining 1 tablespoon olive oil over medium heat until shimmering. Place the halved or quartered bok choy cut-side down and sear until browned, 1 to 2 minutes.

Add most of the cilantro to the soup, reserving some to garnish, and the seared bok choy and cook for 5 more minutes.

Ladle the soup into bowls and garnish with the reserved cilantro. Store any leftovers in an airtight container in the refrigerator for up to 3 days.

Watercress and Corn with White Bean Soup

If I had to pick a favorite bean soup, this one might be it. Clean and fresh yet deceptively hearty, this soup checks all the boxes for me. One of my favorite ways to enjoy watercress is in soup because it wilts down and mellows slightly, muting the peppery notes just a bit. Corn and watercress are a natural pairing because corn's sweetness marries beautifully with watercress's spicy greenness. For this soup, you want to cook the potatoes right to the point where they start breaking down along the outer edges, lending a slight creaminess to the broth, a bit reminiscent of a chowder. When choosing a white bean, go with your favorite; I usually use a flageolet or navy bean. I recommend serving this soup with a mound of steamed white rice in the middle of the bowl. If you're planning on having leftovers, add only enough watercress for your serving. Add more when reheating, as the watercress becomes bitter if left in the soup overnight.

Serves 6

Shiitake Broth

6 dried shiitake mushrooms, rinsed and cleaned to remove debris

6 cups hot water

Soup

3 ears corn, shucked

1 tablespoon unsalted butter

1 tablespoon extra-virgin olive oil

1 sweet onion, diced

2 teaspoons kosher salt, plus more as needed

1 pound Yukon Gold potatoes, peeled and cut into ½-inch cubes

2 garlic cloves, finely grated

2 tablespoons Better Than Bouillon vegetable base

1 tablespoon soy sauce (shoyu)

1 teaspoon freshly ground black pepper

One 1-pound bunch watercress, cut into 2-inch segments

1 teaspoon distilled white vinegar

3 cups cooked Soup Beans (page 65), made with white beans, such as flageolet or navy

1 cup bean cooking broth, plus more to taste

To make the shiitake broth: In a bowl, combine the shiitakes and the hot water and soak for 20 minutes. Scoop out the shiitakes and squeeze the excess liquid back into the bowl. Save the shiitakes for another use. Set the shiitake broth aside.

To make the soup: Cut the corn kernels from the cob and set both the kernels and the cobs aside on a plate or in a bowl.

In a large pot, combine the butter and olive oil and heat over medium heat until shiny. Add the onion and ½ teaspoon of the salt and sauté until the onion is just translucent and fragrant, about 5 minutes.

Add the potatoes and sauté for a few minutes. Add the garlic and cook for 30 seconds, then add the shiitake broth, bouillon base, corn cobs, soy sauce, pepper, and the remaining 1½ teaspoons salt. Stir to combine, then increase the heat to medium-high to bring to a boil. Reduce the heat to medium-low, cover, and simmer until the potatoes start breaking down around the edges, about 50 minutes. Taste the soup and adjust the salt to taste. Remove the corn cobs and compost or discard.

While the soup is simmering, soak the watercress in a bowl of cold water with the vinegar for 5 to 10 minutes. This ensures the watercress is as clean as possible and rehydrates the leaves. Drain and rinse thoroughly.

Add the beans, the bean broth, adding more broth, if desired, and the corn kernels and cook for 15 more minutes.

Start by adding half of the watercress, reserving some of the tenderest leaves for garnish, and adding more depending on your preference. Cook for 5 more minutes.

Ladle the soup into bowls and garnish with the reserved watercress leaves. Store any leftovers in an airtight container in the refrigerator for up to 3 days.

Squash and Pinto Bean Soup

This soup is packed with squash; I like a mix of butternut squash, kabocha, and delicata, but it's the dealer's choice, so use what you love. In addition to lots of squash, which adds sweetness, this soup ditches the signature cozy spice vibe and is finished with a healthy drizzle of your favorite chili crisp and some green onion. If you aren't a heat fan, substitute something milder, like chili onion crunch oil or some crispy onions.

Serves 6

Shiitake Broth

3 dried shiitake mushrooms, rinsed and cleaned to remove debris

3 cups hot water

Soup

1 tablespoon unsalted butter

1 to 2 tablespoons extra-virgin olive oil

1 sweet onion, diced

2 teaspoons kosher salt, plus more as needed

2 carrots, roughly chopped

2 pounds assorted winter squash, peeled (if necessary) and cut into ¾-inch cubes or bite-size pieces

2 garlic cloves, finely grated

1 tablespoon Better Than Bouillon vegetable base

One 14.5-ounce can diced tomatoes

One 8-ounce can tomato sauce

1 tablespoon ketchup

1 tablespoon soy sauce (shoyu)

1 bay leaf

1 teaspoon freshly ground black pepper

3 cups Soup Beans (page 65), made with pinto beans

1 to 1½ cups bean cooking broth, to taste

1 cup coarsely chopped fresh cilantro, plus more for garnish

3 green onions, chopped

Chili crisp, for drizzling

To make the a shiitake broth: In a bowl, combine the shiitakes and the hot water and soak for 20 minutes. Scoop out the shiitakes and squeeze the excess liquid back into the bowl. Save the shiitakes for another use. Set the shiitake broth aside.

To make the soup: In a large pot, combine the butter and 1 tablespoon of the olive oil and heat over medium heat until shiny. Add the onion and ½ teaspoon of the salt and sauté until the onion is just translucent and fragrant, about 5 minutes.

Add the carrots with another ½ teaspoon of the salt and cook for 3 minutes, stirring occasionally, adding another 1 tablespoon olive oil if needed. Add the winter squash and ½ teaspoon of the salt and cook for 5 minutes, stirring a few times. Add the garlic and cook for 30 seconds, then add 2 cups of the shiitake broth, bouillon base, diced tomatoes, tomato sauce, ketchup, soy sauce, bay leaf, pepper, and the remaining ½ teaspoon salt. Stir to combine, then increase the heat to medium-high to bring to a boil. Reduce the heat to medium-low, cover, and simmer until the squash is tender, about 30 minutes. Taste the soup and adjust the salt to taste.

Add the pinto beans bean broth and the remaining 1 cup of shiitake broth to top up the liquid, if needed, and cook for 15 more minutes. Add the cilantro and most of the green onions, reserving some to garnish, and cook for 5 more minutes.

Ladle the soup into bowls and garnish with cilantro, green onions, and a drizzle of chili oil. Store any leftovers in an airtight container in the refrigerator for up to 3 days.

Tofu Burgers Loco Moco

Loco moco is so popular in Hawai'i that you can even find it on menus at local Mexican restaurants (shout-out to Acevedos on Maui). In the simplest terms, loco moco is a burger topped with a silky, umami-rich gravy and a fried egg. On the surface, a tofu burger loco moco might not sound alluring, but it's one of my favorite things to eat. The only thing that takes a bit of extra effort is planning ahead to freeze the tofu. Honestly, frozen tofu is great for stir-frying, deep-frying, soups, and these burgers, so you might want to freeze extra tofu to keep on hand for future recipes. Freezing the tofu transforms it, leaving you with a spongier yet denser texture that can be great for holding sauces, but the tofu also can be pressed to remove extra moisture for things like burgers!

Makes 4 burgers

Burgers

One 12-ounce block firm tofu, frozen (see Note), thawed, and drained

1 carrot, peeled and finely grated

1 tablespoon extra-virgin olive oil

¼ sweet onion, finely minced

1 garlic clove, finely grated

2 large eggs, beaten

½ cup panko bread crumbs

1 tablespoon nutritional yeast

2 tablespoons potato starch or cornstarch

1 tablespoon soy sauce (shoyu)

1 tablespoon Kewpie mayonnaise

Freshly ground black pepper

1 tablespoon neutral oil (see page 18), plus more as needed

For Serving

Brown Gravy (recipe follows)

4 cups cooked rice of your choice

4 large eggs, cooked sunny-side up or over easy

1 green onion, thinly sliced, for garnish

To make the burgers: Start with two bowls, a small and medium bowl. Using your hands, squeeze the liquid from the piece of thawed tofu into the smaller bowl. It will start to crumble as you squeeze, which is good; crumbles are the result you're after. Once you've squeezed the liquid from the tofu, crumble it into the medium bowl.

In batches, squeeze the carrot over the small bowl to release any excess liquid and place the dry carrot into the medium bowl. Repeat until the carrot has been processed. Discard the liquid in the small bowl.

Preheat the oven to 200°F or to "keep warm."

In a large skillet, heat the olive oil over medium heat until shiny. Add the onion and sauté until just translucent, about 5 minutes. Add the garlic and cook for 30 seconds. Remove from the heat and add the onion and garlic to the bowl. Wipe the pan clean and set on the stovetop.

To the bowl, add the eggs, panko, nutritional yeast, potato starch, soy sauce, mayo, and a few cracks of pepper. Mix well. Divide the mixture into 4 equal portions and shape into patties roughly 4 inches wide. For ease of cooking, you can optionally refrigerate the patties for 10 minutes.

Line a small tray with paper towels and have near the stove. Set the skillet over medium heat, add the neutral oil, and heat until shiny. Working in batches if necessary, add the burgers and cook until dark golden brown and set, 4 to 6 minutes per side. Set on the paper towels to rest. Add more oil as needed if you are cooking in batches. Keep warm in the oven.

To serve: Make the brown gravy as directed, but use the skillet you used to cook the burgers. Place 1 cup of rice on a plate and top with (in this order) 1 burger, some gravy, 1 fried egg, and some green onion.

Note: To freeze tofu, all you need to do is drain it, then cut it into whatever shape or size you plan to use later, pop it in a freezer-safe container, and about 6 hours later, you'll have frozen tofu. A slightly yellow color is normal and goes away once you cook it. Thaw tofu overnight in the refrigerator before using it.

Brown Gravy

Makes about 2 cups

1 tablespoon unsalted butter

¼ sweet onion, thinly sliced

4 ounces oyster mushrooms, torn into bite-size pieces

Kosher salt

2 cups hot water

2 teaspoons Better Than Bouillon vegetable base

2 teaspoons soy sauce (shoyu)

1 teaspoon (vegan) Worcestershire sauce

Freshly ground black pepper

2 tablespoons cornstarch

In a skillet, melt the butter over medium heat. Add the onion and mushrooms with a pinch of salt and sauté until very fragrant and translucent, about 10 minutes.

Remove the skillet from the heat. In a measuring cup, whisk the hot water with the bouillon base and add it to the skillet along with the soy sauce, Worcestershire sauce, and a few cracks of pepper. Bring to a simmer over medium heat. Make a slurry by whisking the cornstarch with 2 tablespoons cold water. Slowly stream the slurry into the pan, whisking the entire time. Simmer for a few minutes or until the gravy reaches your desired thickness.

Black Bean Mushroom Burgers Loco Moco

The thing about black bean burgers, and beany burgers in general, is that they're usually a little stodgy. I found a J. Kenji López-Alt recipe on Serious Eats years ago that changed that. It calls for baking your beans for a short period to dehydrate them, therefore solving the soggy burger problem. I've taken his tips and run with them for these burgers.

Makes 4 burgers

Black Bean Mushroom Burgers

One 15-ounce can black beans, drained and rinsed

2 tablespoons extra-virgin olive oil, plus more as needed

1 pound cremini mushrooms, trimmed and finely diced

½ sweet onion, diced

Kosher salt

2 garlic cloves, finely grated

1 cup panko bread crumbs

1 large egg, beaten

2 teaspoons (vegan) Worcestershire sauce

2 teaspoons soy sauce (shoyu)

1 tablespoon Kewpie mayonnaise

Freshly ground black pepper

For Serving

Brown Gravy (page 73)

4 cups cooked rice of your choice

4 large eggs, cooked sunny-side up or over easy

1 green onion, thinly sliced, for garnish

To make the burgers: Preheat the oven to 350°F. Line a quarter-sheet pan with parchment paper.

Pat the beans dry with a clean kitchen towel or paper towel and spread evenly on the lined sheet pan. Bake for 20 minutes; the beans should look dry, and most should have split open. Let cool for 5 minutes. Leave the oven on but reduce the temperature to 200°F.

Transfer the beans to a food processor and pulse until pea-size. (If you don't have a processor, hand-chop the beans into pea-size pieces and transfer to a large bowl.)

Meanwhile, in a large skillet, heat 1 tablespoon of the olive oil over medium heat until shiny. Add the mushrooms and sauté until softened, about 5 minutes. Add the onion with a pinch of salt and sauté until the onion is just translucent, about 5 minutes more. Add the garlic and sauté for another 30 seconds. Transfer to the food processor (or bowl). Wipe the skillet clean with a paper towel.

Add the panko, egg, Worcestershire sauce, soy sauce, mayo, 1 teaspoon kosher salt, and a few cracks of pepper to the food processor (or bowl) and pulse (or mix) until well combined. Divide the mixture into 4 equal portions and shape into patties roughly 4 inches wide. For ease of cooking, you can optionally refrigerate the patties for 10 minutes.

Line a small tray with paper towels and have near the stove. Set the skillet over medium heat, add the remaining 1 tablespoon olive oil, and heat until shiny. Working in batches if necessary, add the burgers and cook until dark brown and set, 4 to 6 minutes per side. Set on the paper towels to rest. Add more oil as needed if you are cooking in batches. Keep warm in the oven.

To serve: Make the brown gravy as directed, but use the skillet you used to cook the burgers. Place 1 cup of rice on a plate and top with (in this order) 1 burger, some gravy, 1 fried egg, and some green onion.

Breadfruit White Bean Burgers Loco Moco

I once had a breadfruit ('ulu) and taro (kalo) burger made by Chef Lisa Villiarimo at a farming convention, and it has stuck with me ever since. It was my first time trying a breadfruit burger, and it was like a lightbulb went off over my head. I knew I wanted to make a version at home with white beans and zucchini and had a clear vision of a hash patty. This is that, my friends, and it is glorious! Topped with silky, rich brown gravy, it screams breakfast for lunch or dinner, depending on when you're serving it. And no shade if you're slinging loco mocos first thing in the morning; I fully support this.

Makes 4 burgers

Breadfruit White Bean Burgers

8 ounces breadfruit ('ulu), steamed (see Note, page 158)

One 15-ounce can cannellini beans, drained and rinsed

½ small zucchini, grated

2 tablespoons neutral oil (see page 18), plus more as needed

½ carrot, peeled and minced

½ sweet onion, minced

Kosher salt

2 garlic cloves, minced

2 large eggs, beaten

½ cup panko bread crumbs

1 tablespoon soy sauce (shoyu)

2 tablespoons Kewpie mayonnaise

Freshly ground black pepper

For Serving

Brown Gravy (page 73)

4 cups cooked rice of your choice

4 large eggs, cooked sunny-side up or over easy

1 green onion, thinly sliced, for garnish

To make the burgers: Set the steamed breadfruit aside to cool.

Preheat the oven to 350°F. Line a quarter-sheet pan with parchment paper.

Pat the beans dry with a clean kitchen towel or paper towel and spread evenly on the lined sheet pan. Bake for 20 minutes; the beans should look dry, and most should have split open. Let cool for 5 minutes. Leave the oven on but reduce the temperature to 200°F.

Meanwhile, squeeze the liquid from the zucchini, either using your hands or a clean kitchen towel, and discard the liquid.

Transfer the beans to a food processor, add the breadfruit, and pulse until pea-size. Add the zucchini. (If you don't have a processor, use a box grater to grate the breadfruit and then hand-chop the beans. Transfer both to a bowl and add the zucchini.)

In a large skillet, heat 1 tablespoon of the oil over medium heat until shiny. Add the carrot and onion with a pinch of salt and sauté until the onion is just translucent, about 5 minutes. Add the garlic and sauté for another minute. Add to the food processor (or bowl). Wipe the skillet clean with a paper towel.

Add the eggs, panko, soy sauce, mayo, and a few cracks of pepper to the food processor (or bowl) and pulse (or mix) until well combined. Divide the mixture into 4 equal portions and shape into patties roughly 4 inches wide. For ease of cooking, you can optionally refrigerate the patties for 10 minutes.

Line a small tray with paper towels and have near the stove. Set the skillet over medium heat, add the remaining 1 tablespoon oil and heat until shiny. Working in batches if necessary, add the burgers and cook until dark golden brown and set, 4 to 6 minutes per side. Set on the paper towels to rest. Add more oil as needed if you are cooking in batches. Keep warm in the oven.

To serve: Make the brown gravy as directed, but use the skillet you used to cook the burgers. Place 1 cup of rice on a plate and top with (in this order) 1 burger, some gravy, 1 fried egg, and some green onion.

Black Lentil Burgers Loco Moco

Molly Baz's lentil burger was the first one I'd ever had, and I immediately thought, Wow. Admittedly, I'm not a veggie burger connoisseur, but lentil burgers have something special going on. They aren't meat, but they are kinda meaty. The earthiness of the lentils cuts through pleasantly, and the ketchup gives it a meatloaf-y vibe (a good thing). And like most burgers, they're great with a solid dose of brown gravy. I mean, there's very little that isn't improved by brown gravy. Black lentils retain their shape and structure more than other types of lentils, so please do not substitute a different type.

Makes 4 burgers

Black Lentil Burgers

½ cup dried black lentils, rinsed

Kosher salt

2 tablespoons extra-virgin olive oil, plus more as needed

½ sweet onion, diced

½ teaspoon smoked paprika

2 garlic cloves, finely minced

One 15-ounce can chickpeas, drained (but not rinsed)

Freshly ground black pepper

1 tablespoon soy sauce (shoyu)

2 tablespoons ketchup

1 tablespoon Kewpie mayonnaise

⅓ cup all-purpose flour, plus more as needed

For Serving

Brown Gravy (page 73)

4 cups cooked rice of your choice

4 large eggs, cooked sunny-side up or over easy

1 green onion, thinly sliced, for garnish

To make the burgers: In a saucepan, combine the lentils, 1 tablespoon salt, and water to cover by a few inches. Bring it to a boil over high heat, then reduce to medium-high and simmer until very tender, 35 to 40 minutes. Drain in a fine-mesh sieve and place in a large bowl.

In a large skillet, heat 1 tablespoon of the olive oil over medium heat until shiny. Add the onion and sauté until softened, about 5 minutes. Add the smoked paprika and garlic and sauté for 30 seconds. Add to the bowl of lentils.

Add the chickpeas to the bowl and mash with a potato masher until the lentils and chickpeas are lightly smashed but not mushy. Add a pinch of salt, a few cracks of pepper, the soy sauce, ketchup, and mayo. Give it a big stir to combine, then add the flour and stir to incorporate evenly. The mixture should be able to hold if you pack it into a patty. Grab a small amount and squeeze; add a tablespoon or two more flour if it doesn't stay together. Divide the mixture into 4 equal portions and shape into patties roughly 4 inches wide. For ease of cooking, you can optionally refrigerate the patties for 10 minutes.

Line a small tray with paper towels and have near the stove. Set the skillet over medium heat, add the remaining 1 tablespoon olive oil, and heat until shiny. Working in batches if necessary, add the burgers and cook until dark brown and set, 4 to 6 minutes per side. Set on the paper towels to rest. Add more oil as needed if you are cooking in batches. Keep warm in the oven.

To serve: Make the brown gravy as directed, but use the skillet you used to cook the burgers. Place 1 cup of rice on a plate and top with (in this order) 1 burger, some gravy, 1 fried egg, and some green onion.

STAUB

Cabbage Adobo with Butternut Squash and Black Lentils

This dish is a banger packed with a punchy braising sauce that's bright from the vinegar and spicy thanks to the pepper. It's filled with tons of textures (read: tender, toothy, creamy). Believe me when I tell you, this dish exceeded my wildest expectations. Based on arguably one of the most famous Filipino dishes, chicken adobo, my vegetable version centers around an acidic, salty braise loaded with garlic and pepper. Make this if you're craving something to warm you up from the inside.

Serves 4 to 6

2 bay leaves

2 teaspoons black peppercorns

4 tablespoons neutral oil (see page 18), plus more as needed

1 head green cabbage (1½ to 2 pounds), trimmed, halved through the core, and cut into 6 wedges

Kosher salt

⅓ cup cane or distilled white vinegar

⅓ cup soy sauce (shoyu)

⅔ cup water

1 tablespoon light brown sugar

6 garlic cloves, smashed and peeled

½ cup dried black lentils, rinsed

½ sweet onion, thinly sliced

½ butternut squash, peeled and seeded

2 green onions, green parts only, sliced on a bias, for garnish

In a Dutch oven, toast the bay leaves and peppercorns over medium heat until very fragrant, 3 to 4 minutes. Remove them from the heat and use a mortar and pestle to crush the peppercorns into a medium-grind size. Set the bay leaves and crushed pepper aside. If you'd like to skip toasting the spices, you can. Set your pepper grinder to medium-grind if you'd like to use it instead.

In the same pan, heat 2 tablespoons of the oil over medium heat and add half the cabbage wedges, cut-side down, sprinkling each wedge with salt to taste, and sear until caramelized and almost charred on both sides, 4 to 5 minutes per side. Add more oil if necessary. Remove the wedges from the pan and sprinkle with more salt to taste. Repeat with the other half of the wedges using the remaining 2 tablespoons oil. Reserve all the wedges on a plate or sheet pan.

In the same pan, combine the cane vinegar, soy sauce, water, brown sugar, garlic cloves, toasted bay leaves, and black pepper. Bring it all to a simmer over medium heat and add the lentils. Nestle the cabbage wedges and the onion slices into the sauce. Increase the heat to medium-high and bring the sauce to a low boil. Reduce the heat to medium-low, cover the pan, and simmer for 30 minutes.

Meanwhile, prepare the squash. Cut in half, from top to bottom, then turn 180 degrees and cut into ⅜-inch-thick pieces.

After 30 minutes of cooking, remove the lid, flip the cabbage wedges, tuck in the sliced butternut squash, cover, and continue simmering until deeply tender, another 30 minutes.

Serve garnished with the green onion.

Note: I could be wrong, but lentils aren't exactly a Hawai'i thing. And by this, I mean there aren't a lot of local Hawai'i dishes (I can't think of any outside of the recipes in this book) that have lentils in them. All this is to say that I was over thirty years old by the time I tried lentils for the first time. They were black lentils, also called beluga or caviar lentils, and I thought this was what all lentils were like. They are not, so please don't substitute other types here.

Japanese Eggplant "Adobo"

You'll note that adobo is in quotes here, and that's definitely intentional. I hesitate to call this eggplant adobo because it's not simmered in the punchy adobo sauce but steamed and dressed in the sauce at the end. This borrows from the Chinese method of steaming eggplant, which I learned from cookbook author Betty Liu, and I think it's a textural revelation. Steaming the eggplant leaves you with a creamy, almost silky texture that can absorb the adobo sauce lightly. This dish is perfect served with Pan-Seared Crispy Rice (page 148), as the chew and crunch of the rice play well with the delicate softness of the eggplant. Not traditional but highly repeatable.

Serves 4

2 Japanese or Chinese eggplants

2 teaspoons kosher salt

2 teaspoons neutral oil (see page 18)

2 garlic cloves, thinly sliced

½ teaspoon freshly ground black pepper

3 green onions, chopped

2 tablespoons cane or distilled white vinegar

2 tablespoons soy sauce (shoyu)

1 teaspoon light brown sugar

Trim the calyx and stems (carefully if they have spines) from the eggplants before slicing them lengthwise in quarters (think end to end) so you have 4 long strips per eggplant. Cut each strip in thirds so you have 12 pieces per eggplant. Place the pieces in a colander set in a bowl or the sink and toss with the salt. Let it sit for 15 minutes before rinsing off the salt.

Pat the eggplant pieces dry with a clean kitchen towel or paper towels and lay them on a towel to dry thoroughly before steaming. You want the eggplant to be as dry as possible to get it creamy and silky versus slimy.

Fit a steamer basket over a large pot or pan filled with water to a height of 2 inches. Remove the basket, replace the lid on the pot, and bring the water to a boil over medium-high heat, then promptly reduce the heat to medium-low to keep at a steady simmer.

Arrange the eggplant pieces skin-side down in the basket, stacking the remaining pieces perpendicular, still skin-side down. (Arranging the eggplant skin-side down is essential to achieving that silky texture.)

Set the basket over the pot, replace the steamer lid, and steam until a knife can be easily inserted into the middle of a piece without resistance, about 20 minutes. Transfer the eggplant to a plate.

Meanwhile, in a small skillet, heat the oil over medium heat until shiny. Add the garlic and sauté until fragrant and softened, 1 to 2 minutes. Add the pepper and two-thirds of the green onions and sauté for a minute. Remove the pan from the heat and add the cane vinegar, soy sauce, and brown sugar. Return the pan to medium heat and cook for 1 minute.

Pour the sauce over the eggplant, garnish with the remaining green onions, and serve.

Daikon Adobo

Daikon is a unique vegetable because it undergoes such a transformation when cooked. When raw, it's crunchy and slightly peppery, but when it's cooked, it becomes this sweet and juicy ethereal thing that I just can't get enough of. I find it pairs beautifully with the acid in adobo. The hardest part about making this dish is cutting the daikon; even that part is a breeze. Make this on a weeknight when you're craving something different. It's on the lighter side, so I suggest serving it with a larger side and some rice. Mushroomy Rice (page 130) is great with this. Note: I used purple daikon in the photo, but normal white daikon works best. Look for smaller daikon that are similar widths.

Serves 4

2 pounds daikon

3 cups water

¼ cup cane or distilled white vinegar

¼ cup soy sauce (shoyu)

3 tablespoons light brown sugar

6 garlic cloves, smashed and peeled

1 teaspoon crushed black peppercorns

1 bay leaf

1 handful chives, finely chopped

Peel the daikon and cut it into 1½-inch-thick disks. Use the peeler to round the cut edges; this helps keep the daikon edges from breaking off while cooking.

In a Dutch oven, wide enough to arrange the daikon in an even layer, arrange the daikon in a single layer and add the water, cane vinegar, soy sauce, brown sugar, garlic, peppercorns, and bay leaf. Bring to a rapid simmer over medium heat, then reduce the heat to low, cover, and gently simmer for 1 hour. The daikon should be tender enough for a knife to cut through the center easily.

Set the lid askew and cook over medium heat until about three-quarters of the liquid has cooked off. Use a spoon to plate the daikon, serving some of the sauce with it. Top with chopped chives.

Backyard Garden

My love for gardening dates back to my early childhood, when my mom let me grow bozu (globe amaranth) and impatiens alongside the beautiful roses in her garden. They, of course, paled in comparison but ignited my love for gardening. To this day, I still love growing flowers, so much so that we've created a cut flower garden in our backyard. I've always marveled at what you can grow when you put a little energy into the earth, but it wasn't until recently that I started to attempt to grow some of my produce.

My husband and I were lucky to get a plot at our community garden, Ocean View Farms, in Mar Vista in 2020. We transformed a weed-addled space into a small oasis of vegetal paradise, spending weeks clearing the weeds and even more time building out beds and pathways in our small space. My enthusiasm for growing was fueled by the times, as this took place near the start of the pandemic. But it was exhilarating to spend so much time outside, growing vegetables that we were excited to try and experimenting with building lean-to trellises.

At the community garden, I met Uncle Warren, one of the most remarkable human beings I've ever met. He was well into his nineties and still tending his plots daily, growing some of the best lettuce heads and carrots I've seen. And what's more, he was initially from Hawai'i, so we felt an instant connection to him (people from Hawai'i, IYKYK). He taught me that compost is your best friend when gardening, and I think of him whenever I add some to my backyard garden. We learned about French intensive gardening from another garden member, a method we inadvertently adopted to grow a lot in our small plot. I was excited to try to grow everything under the sun, so I planted our crops tightly, interplanting and companion planting all over. And you know what? It was so much fun. I had lots of failures but lots of successes. I got really creative with zucchini that year!

Now that we're home in Hawai'i, the pull toward gardening has grown substantially. We live in Kula, and the soil here is super fertile. Most things want to grow here, and I've found that growing from seed is worth the extra effort. Growing my plants from seed allows me to try a greater variety and a wider range of cultivars than when buying the starts from the store. It's also way more cost-effective. I have cases devoted to storing all my seeds, as each season promises another chance to try something new.

I've been growing many Japanese eggplants lately because I love them so much, and once you establish a plant, it booms for a while.

Hakurei turnips, also called salad turnips or Tokyo turnips, have been on repeat because they are fantastic. I have pole beans galore, which give and give until you're up to your ears in them. I continue to seed purple daikon because it's easy to grow and fast; it's also beautiful to cook with. You can grow squash year-round here, though mine get hit with more powdery mildew in the wintry months. The same goes for tomatoes and cucumbers, and I guess most things!

In 2024, Moses and I started a māla (dryland kalo/taro patch) with some huli (cutting) gifted to us from Noho'ana Farm in Waikapū. We also planted a huge row of apple banana plants (mai'a), apple trees, and stone fruit trees. We tried to grow breadfruit ('ulu), but we're too high up, and the tree never took off. The property already had well-established citrus trees and avocados, so we are on our way to creating a tiny food forest. The joy and pride we feel when harvesting our food (and flowers) is one of the main reasons I encourage everyone to try growing at least one thing they consume.

Long Bean Adobo with Oyster Mushrooms and Abura-age

If you haven't seen long beans before, they're hard to picture, but they are generally 1 to 2 feet long, making them genuinely long beans! Sometimes called snake beans, they tend to have thicker skins, lending themselves to braising for a short time. Long bean adobo, adobong sitaw, is traditionally made with pork belly, but I find oyster mushrooms to be so meaty that they pair beautifully with the beans. Abura-age, a deep-fried tofu puff, rounds out the dish to give it some tenderness. If you can't find long beans, don't fret! You can substitute French green beans, but just reduce the cooking time by a few minutes.

Serves 4

2 tablespoons neutral oil (see page 18)

8 ounces oyster mushrooms, torn or cut into 2- to 3-inch lengths

¼ sweet onion, diced

4 garlic cloves, grated

12 ounces long beans, cut into 2-inch lengths

½ teaspoon freshly ground black pepper

¼ cup cane or distilled white vinegar

¼ cup soy sauce (shoyu)

¼ cup water

2 teaspoons light brown sugar

3 ounces abura-age, cut into quarters diagonally

In a large sauté pan with a lid, heat 1 tablespoon of the oil over medium-high heat until shiny. Add the oyster mushrooms and sauté for 5 minutes.

Reduce the heat to medium, add the onion, and cook for 3 minutes, stirring often. Add the garlic, long beans, and pepper and sauté for 2 minutes. Remove the pan from the heat and add the cane vinegar, soy sauce, water, brown sugar, and abura-age. Return the pan to medium heat and bring to a simmer. Cover, reduce the heat to medium-low, and simmer until the beans are tender but still have a slight crunch, 10 to 15 minutes.

Serve immediately.

Classic Mochiko

Give me anything fried, but marinate it in a salty-sweet batter? Forget about it. This dish is a medley of delicious ingredients, fried to perfection, based on my all-time favorite: mochiko chicken. It features a delicately crispy exterior with a variation of textures on the interior, depending on what's on the inside. Varying the shapes and sizes of the components creates some visual texture that goes a long way. This dish can be adapted to use many of the veggies you have on hand. Mochiko chicken is Hawai'i's answer to fried chicken, reflecting the heavy Japanese influence on the local Hawai'i food culture. Vegetable bonus: While the chicken version requires overnight marination, plants require significantly less marinating, 30 minutes at most. I've included various ways to make it—sesame-y!, gingery!, or spicy!—as what to mochiko. My mom will tell you that her new favorite mochiko is gingery mochiko, and that's saying something because the classic mochiko is her recipe!

Serves 4

- ⅓ cup sweet rice flour (mochiko)
- ⅓ cup potato starch
- 3 tablespoons sugar
- ¼ cup soy sauce (shoyu)
- ½ teaspoon kosher salt
- 2 large eggs, beaten
- 2 green onions, chopped, plus more for garnish
- 2 garlic cloves, finely grated
- ½-inch piece fresh ginger, peeled and finely grated
- Roughly 2 pounds veggies of your choice (see What to Mochiko, page 93)
- Neutral oil (see page 18), for deep-frying

In a bowl, whisk together the sweet rice flour, potato starch, sugar, soy sauce, salt, eggs, green onions, garlic, and ginger.

Prepare the vegetables according to What to Mochiko (page 93). Toss them in the marinade and set the bowl in the refrigerator for 15 to 30 minutes to chill and marinate simultaneously.

Line a baking sheet with paper towels and have near the stove. Pour 1½ to 2 inches of oil into a Dutch oven or a deep heavy-bottomed pan and heat over medium heat to 340° to 350°F.

Before frying, make sure the veggies are evenly coated. Working in batches, fry the veggies until golden brown all over, 2 to 3 minutes per side. Transfer to the paper towels to drain. Serve immediately.

continued

Make It...

While the classic mochiko will always be number one in my heart, there's always room for more versions and it's easy to make: Sesame-y!, Spicy!, or Gingery! Simply add the following ingredients to the classic mochiko marinade:

...Sesame-y!

3 tablespoons tahini

2 tablespoons ground sesame seeds

1 tablespoon toasted sesame oil

...Gingery!

Omit the ginger in the Classic Mochiko marinade and instead add

2-inch piece fresh ginger, finely minced

2-inch piece fresh ginger, finely grated

...Spicy!

2 tablespoons gochujang (Korean chile paste)

2 teaspoons gochugaru (Korean chile flakes)

Classic Mochiko, continued

What to Mochiko

This is a list of the vegetables (and tofu) I've found to be the best mochiko'd. We can call them Mochiko MVPs. Feel free to experiment with others, and if you find one that works well, let me know! You'll notice that many require scoring or peeling with a serrated peeler. This gives the surface as much texture as possible to hold the marinade.

Carrots

Cut into ¼-inch-thick pieces or rounds and optionally use a serrated peeler to give the cut sides more texture.

Eggplant

Fairy Tale: Cut in half and lightly score a crosshatch pattern over the cut sides.
Globe: Cut off the stem and calyx, slice into ¼-inch-thick rounds, and lightly score a crosshatch pattern over the cut sides.
Japanese/Chinese: Cut off the stem and calyx, slice on a bias into ¼-inch-thick pieces, and lightly score a crosshatch pattern over the cut sides.

Mushrooms

Button: Slice lengthwise in halves or thirds, depending on the size, and lightly score a crosshatch pattern over the cut sides.
Enoki: Tear into small bunches.
King trumpet: Slice lengthwise into 2 to 4 strips, depending on the size, and lightly score a crosshatch pattern over the cut sides.
Oyster: Keep whole unless the mushrooms are extra large, in which case, tear them into smaller pieces.

Onions

Sweet onion: Cut into ¼-inch-thick rounds and use your hands to pull apart rounds if desired.

Sweet potato (ʻuala)

Scrub the skin, cut into ¼-inch rounds or pieces, and optionally use a serrated peeler to give the cut sides more texture.

Tofu

Firm or extra-firm: Cut into ¼-inch-thick pieces and lightly score a crosshatch pattern over the cut sides.

Winter squash

Delicata: Cut into ¼-inch-thick rounds and scoop out the seeds from each round.
Honeynut: Cut in half lengthwise, scoop out the seeds, then cut into ¼-inch-thick strips.
Kabocha, sweet dumpling, or red kuri: Cut into 2-inch pieces (see page 26 for kabocha cutting tips).

Honorable Mention

Broccoli and Cauliflower

Cut into florets and optionally use a serrated peeler to give the cut sides more texture. Serve these immediately after frying.

Green Bean Jun

My partner Moses's dad makes a lot of meat jun, fish jun, and just jun in general. We grow a lot of green beans, we love them, our dogs love them, and one day, I thought to try to turn them into jun, because what is jun if not something that's thinly sliced, marinated, battered in egg, and pan-fried? But when Moses told his dad I was making green bean jun, he said, "Oh, Grandma Aipa used to make that, but she would thread them together with a skewer!" This version is a little easier than Grandma Aipa's and hopefully just as tasty.

Makes 4 pancakes

¼ cup soy sauce (shoyu)

3 tablespoons light brown sugar

2 teaspoons toasted sesame oil

2 garlic cloves, finely grated

½-inch piece fresh ginger, peeled and finely grated

¼ teaspoon freshly ground black pepper

8 ounces green beans, trimmed and thinly sliced on a bias

1 small sweet onion, thinly sliced

For Serving

4 large eggs

Kosher salt

Neutral oil (see page 18), for frying

Dipping Sauce (recipe follows)

In a bowl, whisk together the soy sauce, brown sugar, sesame oil, garlic, ginger, and pepper. Add the green beans and onion to the bowl and toss to coat evenly. Marinate for 20 to 30 minutes at room temperature.

When ready to serve: In a bowl, whisk the eggs with a pinch of salt until smooth. Set aside.

In a small nonstick skillet, heat 2 teaspoons oil over medium heat until shimmering. Using tongs, add one-quarter of the green bean/onion mixture to the pan, shaking off the excess marinade into the bowl. Using a flat silicone spatula, stir-fry until the onion softens, 4 to 5 minutes. Use the spatula to flatten the mixture into an even layer that fills the entire pan.

Pour one-quarter of the beaten eggs into the pan, starting from the middle of the pan and working your way out so that you evenly coat the bean mixture. Use the spatula to distribute any excess egg in the pan so that it's as even as possible and cook undisturbed until well set, 3 to 4 minutes. Use the spatula to loosen the egg from the skillet, working around the sides, shaking the pan as necessary. Flip the pancake over either with the help of the spatula or, if you're brave, with a flick of the wrist. Cook until well set, 2 to 3 minutes. Repeat to make the remaining jun.

Cut each pancake into wedges and serve warm with the dipping sauce.

Dipping Sauce

Makes around ½ cup

⅓ cup soy sauce (shoyu)

2 tablespoons rice vinegar

1½ teaspoons toasted sesame oil

⅜ teaspoon gochugaru (Korean chile flakes)

1½ teaspoons gochujang (Korean chile paste)

In a small bowl, whisk together the soy sauce, vinegar, sesame oil, gochugaru, and gochujang.

Zucchini Jun

Slicing the zucchini into thin strips versus coins gives this dish a little more visual interest and brings it closer to the classic meat jun strips. The strips are more delicate than coins, so if you're concerned you might have trouble working with them, cut the zucchini into rounds instead. Either way, you'll be left with a tender, meaty zucchini jun!

Serves 4

1 pound zucchini (3 medium zucchini)

Kosher salt

¼ cup soy sauce (shoyu)

3 tablespoons light brown sugar

2 teaspoons toasted sesame oil

2 garlic cloves, finely grated

½-inch piece fresh ginger, peeled and finely grated

¼ teaspoon freshly ground black pepper

For Serving

½ cup all-purpose flour

4 large eggs

Kosher salt

Neutral oil (see page 18), for frying

Dipping Sauce (page 95)

Cut the zucchini lengthwise into ⅓-inch-thick strips. Place them in a bowl and lightly salt each piece. Let it sit for about 10 minutes to soften and release moisture. Pat each slice dry to remove excess moisture.

In a large bowl, whisk together the soy sauce, brown sugar, sesame oil, garlic, ginger, and pepper. Add the zucchini to the bowl and toss gently to coat evenly. Marinate for 15 to 20 minutes at room temperature, tossing a few times to ensure even marination.

When ready to serve: Place the flour in a shallow bowl. In another shallow bowl, whisk the eggs with a pinch of salt until smooth.

Line a plate with paper towels and have near the stove. In a large skillet, heat 2 tablespoons oil over medium heat until shimmering. Working in batches, dredge the zucchini, one piece at a time, in the flour, shaking off the excess, then dip it into the egg, letting the excess drip off before placing each piece in the skillet. Fry until golden on both sides, 2 to 3 minutes per side. Transfer to the paper towels to drain.

Serve warm with the dipping sauce.

Yuba, Cabbage, and Sweet Potato Jun

This is reminiscent of an oyakodon, a Japanese rice bowl that features chicken and veggies simmered in a soy dashi (broth) with egg. It also reminds me of an okonomiyaki, a savory Japanese pancake that commonly contains cabbage and is cooked on a teppan (grill). It feels very Hawai'i to have a dish that blends a few different food memories to create one dish, as many of our dishes have more than one cultural influence woven into them. This dish uses yuba strips, also known as tofu skins, which are the delicate layers that form on the top of soy milk as it cooks. Here it's served with Kimchi Carrot Fried Rice (page 146) and Shoyu Onion Quickle (page 167).

Makes 4 pancakes

¼ cup soy sauce (shoyu)

3 tablespoons light brown sugar

2 teaspoons toasted sesame oil

2 garlic cloves, finely grated

½-inch piece fresh ginger, peeled and finely grated

¼ teaspoon freshly ground black pepper

5 ounces fresh yuba sheets, cut into ¼-inch-wide strips

½ small head green cabbage, cored and shredded

1 small sweet potato, peeled and shredded

For Serving

6 large eggs

Kosher salt

Neutral oil (see page 18), for frying

2 green onions, thinly sliced

Dipping Sauce (page 95)

In a large bowl, whisk together the soy sauce, brown sugar, sesame oil, garlic, ginger, and pepper. Add the yuba, cabbage, and sweet potato and toss to coat evenly. Marinate for 20 to 30 minutes at room temperature, tossing a few times to ensure even marination.

When ready to serve: In a shallow bowl, whisk the eggs with a pinch of salt until smooth. Set aside.

In a large skillet, heat 2 tablespoons oil over medium heat until shimmering. Using tongs, add the cabbage mixture to the pan, shaking off any excess marinade into the bowl. Using a spatula or wooden spoon, stir-fry until the sweet potato is cooked through and the cabbage has softened, 5 to 7 minutes.

In a small nonstick skillet, heat 1 teaspoon oil over medium heat. Add one-quarter of the stir-fried cabbage mixture. Pour one-quarter of the beaten eggs into the pan, starting from the middle of the pan and working your way out so that you evenly coat the cabbage mixture. Use the spatula to distribute any excess egg in the pan so that it's as even as possible and cook undisturbed until well set, 3 to 4 minutes. Sprinkle one-quarter of the green onions over the top. Use the spatula to loosen the egg from the skillet, working around the sides, shaking the pan as necessary. Flip the pancake over either with the help of the spatula or, if you're brave, with a flick of the wrist. Cook until well set, 2 to 3 minutes. Repeat to make the remaining jun.

Cut each pancake into wedges and serve warm with the dipping sauce.

Oyster Mushroom Jun

This recipe relies on the size of your mushrooms to make larger jun, so look for the biggest oyster mushrooms you can find. Flattening the mushrooms before you marinate them gives the optical illusion of meat. Of all the juns in this book, I'd say this one comes the closest to meat jun, so if you're wondering where to start, this might be the one to try!

Serves 4

Neutral oil (see page 18), for frying

1 pound large oyster mushrooms, caps only

¼ cup soy sauce (shoyu)

3 tablespoons light brown sugar

2 teaspoons toasted sesame oil

2 garlic cloves, finely grated

½-inch piece fresh ginger, peeled and finely grated

¼ teaspoon freshly ground black pepper

For Serving

½ cup all-purpose flour

4 large eggs

Kosher salt

Neutral oil (see page 18), for frying

Dipping Sauce (page 95)

In a large skillet, heat 1 tablespoon neutral oil over medium-high heat until shiny. Add as many mushrooms as you can fit without overlapping them in the pan. Weight the mushrooms down with another slightly smaller skillet or pan to flatten them. Cook for 2 minutes, then remove the pan, flip the mushrooms over, and cook, uncovered, for another 2 minutes. Transfer to a plate. Repeat this process until you've flattened all the mushrooms.

In a bowl, whisk together the soy sauce, brown sugar, sesame oil, garlic, ginger, and pepper. Add the mushrooms and toss to coat evenly. Marinate for 15 to 20 minutes at room temperature, tossing a few times to ensure even marination.

When ready to serve: Place the flour in a shallow bowl. In another shallow bowl, whisk the eggs with a pinch of salt until smooth.

Line a plate with paper towels and have it near the stove. In a large skillet, heat 2 tablespoons neutral oil over medium heat until shimmering. Working in batches, dredge the mushrooms, one piece at a time, in the flour, shaking off the excess, then dip it into the egg, letting the excess drip off before placing each piece in the skillet. Fry until golden all over, 2 to 3 minutes per side. Transfer to the paper towels to drain.

Serve warm with the dipping sauce.

Soft Tofu with Watercress Chinese-Style

Growing up, I'd eat soft tofu with grated ginger, green onions, and soy sauce. Soft tofu is sometimes called silken tofu, and while this book calls for both, I think of soft tofu as the one in the refrigerator section and silken tofu as the one you can find in a box in the Asian foods aisle of the grocery store. This Chinese-style soft tofu—with a beautiful shoyu-infused sauce teeming with ginger, green onions, and cilantro—isn't far from what I used to have, but it feels fancier, more like a treat. The tofu is pulled straight from the refrigerator, giving you a refreshing mix of hot sauce and cold tofu. The hot oil sauce gently wilts the watercress, still leaving the signature crunch but softening it a touch. If you're in Hawai'i, look for Aloha Tofu Soft Tofu—just a heads-up, the block is a little bit bigger, 19 ounces, so don't waste your time looking for a 14-ounce block.

Serves 2

One 14-ounce block soft tofu (refrigerated)

2 teaspoons toasted sesame oil

2 tablespoons soy sauce (shoyu)

1 teaspoon sugar

½ Hawaiian chile pepper (nīoi) or Thai bird's-eye chile (optional), thinly sliced

2 ounces watercress, trimmed and chopped into 2-inch lengths

2-inch piece fresh ginger, peeled and finely julienned

2 green onions, thinly sliced on a bias

½ bunch cilantro, coarsely chopped

2 tablespoons macadamia nut oil or a neutral oil (see page 18) of your choice

Line a quarter-sheet pan with paper towels and carefully invert the tofu from the package onto the paper towels to drain while you prepare the sauce.

In a small bowl, whisk together the sesame oil, soy sauce, sugar, and Hawaiian chile (if using). Set aside.

Carefully arrange the tofu block on a plate. Place the watercress on top, followed by half the ginger, green onions, and cilantro.

In a small saucepan, heat the macadamia nut oil over medium-high heat just until it starts to sizzle. Add the remaining ginger and let it sizzle for 30 seconds, stirring constantly to ensure it doesn't burn. Add the remaining green onions and cilantro and reduce the heat to medium. Carefully add the shoyu sauce mixture and let it cook for 30 seconds.

Pour the sauce over the tofu and serve immediately.

Sumida Farm

Location
'Aiea, O'ahu, Hawai'i

Farm Stats
10 acres
9-foot elevation

Growing
Watercress

Founded
1928

Managers
Kyle and Emi (Sumida) Suzuki, fourth generation

Our farm's purpose is to care for the land to provide the community peace, comfort, education, and nourishment. Take care of the land, take care of the people, and they will take care of the watercress. —Kyle Suzuki

I have always loved watercress, and Sumida Farm grows the best I've ever had. In Hawai'i, Sumida Farm is synonymous with watercress (and for good reason), so I've always just called it Sumida Farm's watercress. In 1928 Moriichi and Makiyo Sumida began growing watercress on five acres of Kalauao Springs land, a source of nourishment for Hawaiian people for more than a millennium, which the Sumidas leased from Kamehameha Schools. Since then, the farm has doubled in size, and while the farm has grown a number of crops over the decades, the Sumidas decided in the '80s that watercress is what grows best in the spring water–fed land. They now grow and harvest over 80 percent of the islands' local watercress supply.

Sumida Farm believes in taking care of the community, so much so that they only distribute in Hawai'i. To them, nourishing their community is vital. In fact, they think of their farm not as a family farm but rather as a community farm. They strive to preserve the land in hopes that it provides a sense of place for locals; when places and things change quickly, the farm serves as an anchor. Located right by a local mall, the farm is a calming sea of green, life, and growth fed by the Kalauao Springs. It embodies our future, present, and past. Today, the farm looks much as it did over fifteen years ago when I first beheld it (on the way to the mall). Their steadfast commitment to serving their community comes through in all that they do.

TEXACO

Broccolini Chinese-Style

I've always pan-fried my broccolini, mainly because it's fast, but my friend Natasha taught me how to roast it, and I've never looked back. There's something about the balance between the super-crispy edges of the florets and the delicate tenderness of the stems that makes this dish extra memorable and, therefore, craveable. Thin, thin slices of lemon add an unexpected brightness. Paired with the aromatic and umami-rich sauce and served atop a creamy butter bean puree, this dish is a treat.

Serves 4

Butter Bean Puree (from Shoyu-Roasted Carrots, page 29; see Note)

2 bunches broccolini or baby broccoli (8 ounces), ends trimmed

½ lemon, thinly sliced into ⅛-inch or thinner half-moons

2 tablespoons extra-virgin olive oil

Kosher salt

2 teaspoons toasted sesame oil

2 tablespoons soy sauce (shoyu)

1 teaspoon sugar

½ Hawaiian chile (nīoi) or Thai bird's-eye chile (optional), thinly sliced

2-inch piece fresh ginger, peeled and finely julienned

2 green onions, thinly sliced on a bias

½ bunch cilantro, coarsely chopped

2 tablespoons macadamia nut oil or a neutral oil (see page 18) of your choice

Preheat the oven to 425°F.

Make the butter bean puree as directed and keep warm on low in a saucepan with the lid on.

Place the broccolini and lemon slices on a half-sheet pan and drizzle with the olive oil, then add a pinch of salt. Toss everything together with your hands, evenly coating the broccolini with the olive oil. Roast until the florets look crispy on the edges and the stems are just cooked through, 12 to 14 minutes.

Meanwhile, in a small bowl, whisk together the sesame oil, soy sauce, sugar, and Hawaiian chile (if using). Set aside.

Spoon the butter bean puree onto a plate, using the back of your spoon to spread it. Place the broccolini with the lemon on top of the puree, leaving behind any excess oil. Place half the ginger, green onions, and cilantro on the broccolini.

In a small saucepan, heat the macadamia nut oil over medium-high heat just until it starts to sizzle. Add the remaining ginger and let it sizzle for 30 seconds, stirring constantly to ensure it doesn't burn. Add the remaining green onions and cilantro and reduce the heat to medium. Carefully add the shoyu sauce and let it cook for 30 seconds.

Pour the sauce over the broccolini and serve immediately.

Note: To roast the garlic for the bean puree, set the head of garlic on a small piece of foil, pour 1 tablespoon extra-virgin olive oil over the exposed cloves, and sprinkle with ¼ teaspoon kosher salt. Wrap the foil tightly around the head of garlic and roast in a 400°F oven for 40 minutes.

Roasted Eggplant with Macadamia Nuts Chinese-Style

Eggplant is such an excellent vegetable to prepare Chinese-style. The crosshatch pattern creates the perfect nooks and crannies for the sauce to seep into, leading to intensely flavorful bites. The toasted macadamia nuts add a crunchy contrast to the tender eggplant and welcome buttery nuttiness.

Serves 4

2 globe eggplants

Kosher salt

Extra-virgin olive oil, for brushing

1 cup unsalted roasted macadamia nuts

2 teaspoons toasted sesame oil

2 tablespoons soy sauce (shoyu)

1 teaspoon sugar

½ Hawaiian chile (nīoi) or Thai bird's eye-chile (optional), thinly sliced

2-inch piece fresh ginger, peeled and finely julienned

2 green onions, thinly sliced on a bias

½ bunch cilantro, coarsely chopped

2 tablespoons macadamia nut oil or a neutral oil (see page 18) of your choice

Preheat the oven to 400°F.

Cut each eggplant in half lengthwise through the stem and calyx and score the cut sides with a crosshatch pattern to create more surface for the salt to penetrate and later for the sauce to seep into. Sprinkle the cut sides with salt and let sit for 15 minutes. Rinse off the salt, pat dry with a clean kitchen towel or paper towels, and lay the eggplant halves on a towel to dry thoroughly.

Brush each cut side with 1 to 2 teaspoons olive oil, then arrange them cut-side down on a half-sheet pan. Roast until the eggplants look like they have collapsed in on themselves, 35 to 40 minutes. During the last 5 minutes of cooking, put the macadamia nuts on a quarter-sheet pan and roast in the oven with the eggplant. Remove both pans at the same time.

Meanwhile, in a small bowl, whisk together the sesame oil, soy sauce, sugar, and Hawaiian chile (if using). Set aside.

Carefully arrange the eggplants on a plate (they're now very tender), cut-side up. Crush the macadamia nuts on a cutting board with the underside of a jar and place them on the eggplants. Place half the ginger, green onions, and cilantro on the eggplants.

In a small saucepan, heat the macadamia nut oil over medium-high heat just until it starts to sizzle. Add the remaining ginger and let it sizzle for 30 seconds, stirring constantly to ensure it doesn't burn. Add the remaining green onions and cilantro and reduce the heat to medium. Carefully add the shoyu sauce mixture and let it cook for 30 seconds.

Pour the sauce over the eggplants and serve immediately.

Sugar Snap Peas Chinese-Style

The key to this dish is lightly kissing the sugar snap peas with some heat, knowing they'll cook down a little more when you pour on the sauce. The snap that gives these peas their name is an essential component of this dish, so err on the side of caution when you're sautéing; less is more. A beautiful melding of flavors and textures happens when you pour the sauce over the peas and the whipped tofu. One suggestion: This dish is excellent topped with Quinoa Crispies (page 150).

Serves 4

Whipped Tofu (page 26)

2 teaspoons toasted sesame oil

2 tablespoons soy sauce (shoyu)

1 teaspoon sugar

½ Hawaiian chile (nīoi) or Thai bird's-eye chile (optional), thinly sliced

2 tablespoons extra-virgin olive oil

1 pound sugar snap peas, trimmed

Kosher salt

2-inch piece fresh ginger, peeled and finely julienned

2 green onions, thinly sliced on a bias

½ bunch cilantro, coarsely chopped

2 tablespoons macadamia nut oil or a neutral oil (see page 18) of your choice

Make the whipped tofu as directed.

In a small bowl, whisk together the sesame oil, soy sauce, sugar, and Hawaiian chile (if using). Set aside.

In a large skillet, heat the olive oil over medium-high heat until shiny. Add the sugar snap peas with a pinch of salt and sauté until they are bright green and start wrinkling slightly on the edges, 2 to 3 minutes.

Spoon the whipped tofu onto a plate, arrange the sugar snap peas on top, and top with half the ginger, green onions, and cilantro.

In a small saucepan, heat the macadamia nut oil over medium-high heat just until it starts to sizzle. Add the remaining ginger and let it sizzle for 30 seconds, stirring constantly to ensure it doesn't burn. Add the remaining green onions and cilantro and reduce the heat to medium. Carefully add the shoyu sauce mixture and let it cook for 30 seconds.

Pour the sauce over the peas and serve immediately.

Sweet Potato and Black Bean Lūʻau Stew

When it comes to lūʻau (taro leaf) stew, there are generally two teams: team sweet and team savory. The sweet version is usually made with coconut milk and a little sugar, while the savory lūʻau usually has only water or some kind of stock or broth. I have enough room in my heart for both, but I find myself craving the sweeter version most. Lūʻau stew is made how you might suspect, by stewing lūʻau, usually with some kind of animal protein. The most common are heʻe (octopus)—funnily enough called squid lūʻau—and beef. This version leans heavily into the sweet notes of coconut. If you're looking for a speedier method using the pressure cooker, please refer to Cremini Ginger Lūʻau Stew (page 116) for cooking times.

Serves 4 to 6

2 pounds taro leaves (lūʻau)

2 teaspoons Hawaiian salt (ʻalaea)

1 tablespoon neutral oil (see page 18)

1 tablespoon unsalted butter

1 sweet onion, thinly sliced

Kosher salt

2 garlic cloves, finely grated

One 13.5-ounce can full-fat coconut milk

1 tablespoon light brown sugar, plus more as needed

2 teaspoons soy sauce (shoyu)

1 tablespoon Better Than Bouillon vegetable base

1½ pounds Okinawan sweet potatoes, peeled and cut into 1-inch pieces

One 15-ounce can black beans, drained and rinsed

Put on some gloves if your skin is sensitive. Wash the taro leaves well and shake off the excess water. With a paring knife, remove the thick center stem. Stack a few leaves at a time and cut them in half width- and lengthwise. Stack again, roll into a large cigar, and cut into 1-inch-wide strips. Repeat until all the leaves have been processed.

Place the leaves in a large pot with the Hawaiian salt and fill with water to cover. Bring it to a boil, then reduce the heat to medium-low and simmer for 2 hours 30 minutes, stirring the leaves in a J motion every 15 minutes to ensure they cook evenly and to keep them from burning on the bottom of the pot. Add more water as needed.

Drain the leaves in a colander. Rinse and dry the pot.

Set the pot over medium heat, add the oil and butter, and heat until the butter is melted. Add the onion and a pinch of kosher salt and sauté until the onion is just translucent and fragrant, about 5 minutes. Add the garlic and sauté for 30 seconds. Return the cooked leaves to the pot and add the coconut milk, brown sugar, soy sauce, bouillon base, sweet potatoes, and water as needed to cover completely with liquid. Cook over medium-low heat for 1 hour 15 minutes more, stirring every 15 minutes with the J motion.

When you have 15 minutes left for the stew, add the black beans and adjust the kosher salt and sugar to taste. Serve in bowls.

Swiss Chard Lū'au Stew with Japanese Turnips and Black Lentils

The thing about leafy greens is that they take up a lot of space in their raw form. But when they hit the heat, they shrink down almost immediately, turning what seems like a mountain of greens into a small molehill. The Swiss chard cooks down faster than lū'au (taro leaf), giving off the same general mouthfeel and earthiness. It's not quite like taro leaf, but it satisfies the craving. It's also a great option if you live where taro leaves are hard to come by. The sweetness in the Swiss chard pairs beautifully with the turnips that melt into the stew.

Serves 4 to 6

2 pounds Swiss chard

2 teaspoons Hawaiian salt ('alaea)

1 tablespoon neutral oil (see page 18)

1 tablespoon unsalted butter

1 sweet onion, thinly sliced

Kosher salt

2 garlic cloves, finely grated

1½ pounds Japanese (Tokyo/Hakurei) turnips, cut into bite-size pieces

½ cup dried black lentils, rinsed

One 13.5-ounce can full-fat coconut milk

1 cup water

2 teaspoons soy sauce (shoyu)

1 tablespoon light brown sugar, plus more as needed

1 tablespoon Better Than Bouillon vegetable base

Trim the stems off the Swiss chard leaves. Stack a few Swiss chard leaves at a time and cut them in half width- and lengthwise. Stack again, roll into a large cigar, and cut into 1-inch-wide strips. Repeat until all the leaves have been processed.

Place the leaves in a large pot with the Hawaiian salt and fill with water to cover. Bring it to a boil, then reduce the heat to medium-low and simmer for 15 minutes, stirring the leaves in a J motion a few times to ensure they cook evenly.

Drain the leaves in a colander. Rinse and dry the pot.

Set the pot over medium heat, add the oil and butter, and heat until the butter is melted. Add the onion and a pinch of kosher salt and sauté until the onion is just translucent and fragrant, about 5 minutes. Add the garlic and sauté for 30 seconds. Add the turnips and cook for 5 minutes.

Return the chard leaves to the pot, add the lentils, coconut milk, water, soy sauce, brown sugar, bouillon base, and more water as needed to cover completely with liquid. Cook over medium-low heat for 1 hour, stirring every 15 minutes with the J motion. Add more water if it looks dry.

Adjust the kosher salt and sugar to taste. Serve in bowls.

Cremini Ginger Lū'au Stew with Shoyu Mushrooms

This recipe employs an alternative cooking method, utilizing a pressure cooker to reduce the cooking time. This stew skews savory, replacing the coconut milk with an umami-filled shiitake broth instead. If you prefer cooking on the stovetop or don't have a pressure cooker, please refer to Sweet Potato and Black Bean Lū'au Stew (page 112) for cooking times.

Serves 4 to 6

Shiitake Broth

4 dried shiitake mushrooms, rinsed and cleaned to remove debris

2½ cups hot water

Stew

2 pounds taro leaves (lū'au)

2 teaspoons Hawaiian salt ('alaea)

2 tablespoons neutral oil (see page 18)

1 tablespoon unsalted butter

10 ounces cremini mushrooms, trimmed and sliced

1 sweet onion, thinly sliced

2-inch piece fresh ginger, peeled and finely minced

Kosher salt

2 garlic cloves, finely grated

1 tablespoon soy sauce (shoyu)

1 tablespoon Better Than Bouillon vegetable base

Shoyu Mushrooms (page 173)

To make the shiitake broth: In a bowl, combine the shiitakes and the hot water and soak for 20 minutes. Scoop out the shiitakes and squeeze the excess liquid back into the bowl. Cut off any tough stems and thinly slice the shiitake mushrooms, then return them to the shiitake broth and set aside.

Meanwhile, to make the stew: Put on some gloves if your skin is sensitive. Wash the lū'au leaves well and shake off the excess water. With a paring knife, remove the thick center stem. Stack a few lū'au leaves at a time and cut them in half width- and lengthwise. Stack again, roll into a large cigar, and cut into 1-inch-wide strips. Repeat until all the leaves have been processed.

Place the leaves into a pressure cooker pot with the Hawaiian salt and fill with water to cover. Seal the pot and cook on high pressure for 20 minutes. Let the pressure release naturally for 15 minutes, then quick-release the rest of the pressure.

Drain the leaves in a colander. Rinse and dry the pot.

Return the pot to the cooker. Set it to sauté, add the oil and butter, and heat until the butter has melted. Add the cremini mushrooms and sauté until the mushrooms are browned, about 8 minutes.

Add the onion, ginger, and a pinch of kosher salt and sauté until the onion is softened, about 5 minutes. Add the garlic and cook for 30 seconds before adding the reserved shiitake broth with the shiitakes, the soy sauce, and bouillon base.

Make the shoyu mushrooms as directed.

Seal the pressure cooker and cook on high pressure for 30 minutes. Let the pressure release naturally for 15 minutes, then quick-release the rest of the pressure if needed. Adjust the kosher salt as needed and serve in bowls.

Spinach Lūʻau Stew with Sesame-Crusted Tofu

This dish was inspired by one that Moses, my partner, and I had at Chef Ed Kenney's Mud Hen Water in Kaimuki, Oʻahu: fresh catch (fish) and lūʻau. Chef Kenney serves up his pan-fried fish and lūʻau for brunch, with some roasted veggies and poached eggs. The tofu in this recipe is quickly marinated, dredged in some cornstarch and sesame seeds, and pan-fried for the ultimately umami-rich, meaty tofu steaks. This spinach version of luʻau cooks in a fraction of the time of taro leaves (lūʻau) and is sure to satisfy your craving for traditional lūʻau stew even when you can't find taro leaves. Look for the big 1-pound clamshells when buying the spinach.

Serves 4 to 6

¼ cup water

2 pounds fresh baby spinach, coarsely chopped

1 tablespoon neutral oil (see page 18)

1 tablespoon unsalted butter

1 sweet onion, thinly sliced

Kosher salt

2 garlic cloves, finely grated

One 13.5-ounce can full-fat coconut milk

1 tablespoon light brown sugar, plus more as needed

2 teaspoons soy sauce (shoyu)

Sesame-Crusted Tofu

2 cups boiling water

Kosher salt

One 12-ounce block firm tofu, drained, cut crosswise into 8 pieces

3 tablespoons soy sauce (shoyu)

1½ tablespoons maple syrup

2 garlic cloves, finely grated

⅛-inch piece fresh ginger, peeled and finely grated

Neutral oil (see page 18), for frying

¼ cup cornstarch

Freshly ground black pepper

⅓ cup sesame seeds (white or black, or a combination)

Flaky salt, for finishing

Pour the water into a large pot and set over medium heat. Add the spinach and use a pair of tongs to toss and move it around so it cooks evenly and doesn't burn. Cook until all the spinach is wilted, 2 to 3 minutes. Transfer to a bowl, draining any liquid, and set aside.

Wipe the pot clean, set it over medium heat, and add the oil and butter. Heat until the butter has melted, then add the onion and a pinch of salt and sauté until the onion is just translucent and fragrant, about 5 minutes.

Add the garlic and sauté for 30 seconds, then return the spinach to the pot and add the coconut milk, brown sugar, and soy sauce. Bring it to a simmer, then reduce the heat to medium-low and cook for 30 to 40 minutes, stirring every 5 to 10 minutes with a J motion.

To make the tofu: In a bowl, combine the boiling water, 2 tablespoons salt, and the tofu. Let it sit for 10 minutes, then drain and pat the tofu dry with a clean kitchen towel or paper towels.

In a medium bowl, whisk together the soy sauce, maple syrup, garlic, and ginger. Add the tofu and marinate for 15 minutes, turning the pieces halfway through.

Line a plate with paper towels and have near the stove. In a large skillet, heat 3 tablespoons oil over medium heat until shiny.

While the oil is heating, set up a dredging station in two shallow bowls: In the first bowl, combine the cornstarch, a pinch of salt, and a few cracks of pepper. In the second bowl, add the sesame seeds.

Dredge each piece of tofu in the cornstarch, then in the sesame seeds. Working in batches, place the tofu in the skillet and fry until golden brown and crispy, 3 to 5 minutes per side. Transfer the fried tofu to the paper towels. Add more oil as needed for the remaining batches. Wipe any excess oil out of the pan with a paper towel and reserve. Finish with a sprinkle of flaky salt.

Adjust the sugar and salt to taste to the spinach. Serve in bowls with a piece or two of sesame crusted tofu on top.

Furikake-Roasted Cauliflower

Furikake-baked salmon is a popular, quick, and easy local Hawai'i dinner option. The salmon is roasted in the oven with a healthy schmear of mayonnaise and a generous sprinkling of furikake. Typically served with steamed white rice and roasted seasoned seaweed snacks, it's a cross between baked sushi, where the sushi rice is covered with toppings and a mayonnaise-based sauce like spicy mayo (or just straight mayo), and a handroll, where you essentially roll your sushi into a small roll that you can pick up and eat with your hands. Here, you build your mini roll by placing some rice and some of the salmon, or in this case, cauliflower, in a seaweed snack. A very tender, melty cauliflower is crucial for this dish to work, so while it may be tempting, please don't skip boiling the cauliflower first—this is the key to those melty stems!

Serves 4

1 large head cauliflower

2 tablespoons kosher salt

3 tablespoons extra-virgin olive oil

3 tablespoons Kewpie mayonnaise

1 teaspoon fresh lemon juice

1 teaspoon wasabi paste

3 tablespoons furikake

Cooked rice of your choice, for serving

One 0.6-ounce package roasted seasoned nori sheets, for serving

Line a baking sheet with paper towels and have near the stove. Trim the stem of the cauliflower, leaving the outer leaves attached if they are in good shape, to create an even flat base. Cut it in half through the stem. Bring a large pot of water to boil over high heat and add the salt. Add the cauliflower and boil, reducing the heat to medium-high, for 5 minutes. Then, immediately remove the cauliflower and place on the paper towels to dry for 20 minutes.

Preheat the oven to 425°F.

Set the cauliflower halves on a quarter-sheet pan and drizzle 1½ tablespoons of the olive oil on the floret side, using your hands to evenly distribute it, then flip it over and drizzle the remaining 1½ tablespoons olive oil on the cut side, again using your hands to distribute the oil evenly.

Roast, cut-side up, for 20 minutes. Flip the cauliflower halves over and roast cut-side down for 10 minutes.

Meanwhile, in a small bowl, mix together the mayo, lemon juice, and wasabi.

Brush the mayo mixture onto the cauliflower florets and stem, getting as much of the mayo into the crevices as possible. Sprinkle the furikake on top and roast for another 10 minutes.

Remove from the oven and serve with your choice of rice and roasted seasoned nori. Use your hands to build little sushi handrolls. You can use a knife to cut the cauliflower into pieces or simply break a piece off with the nori.

Furikake-Broiled Eggplant

Just as quick as furikake-baked salmon, this furikake-broiled eggplant is a super-quick option for a weekday or night. You can grab the flesh using the seaweed or cut it into bite-size pieces to enjoy with the skin on. Either way, this is a fast and fun meal!

Serves 4

3 large Japanese or Chinese eggplants

3 tablespoons extra-virgin olive oil

¼ cup Kewpie mayonnaise

1¼ teaspoons fresh lemon juice

1¼ teaspoons wasabi paste

3 tablespoons furikake

1 green onion, thinly sliced, for serving

Cooked rice of your choice, for serving

One 0.6-ounce package roasted seasoned nori sheets, for serving

Set an oven rack 5 inches below the heating element and turn the broiler on high.

If there are spines, remove the calyx and stem of the eggplants. Cut the eggplants in half lengthwise, then score the cut sides with a crosshatch pattern. Rub each half with 1½ teaspoons of olive oil, coating the skin and cut sides evenly. Set on a half-sheet pan skin-side up.

Broil for 5 minutes, or until the skin is lightly charred and softened.

Meanwhile, in a small bowl, mix together the mayo, lemon juice, and wasabi.

Flip the eggplants and broil for 3 minutes, then brush the mayo over the cut sides. Broil for 1 to 2 more minutes, watching closely to ensure they don't burn. Remove from the oven and sprinkle with the furikake, followed by green onions.

Serve with your choice of rice and roasted seasoned nori. Use your hands to build little sushi handrolls.

Spicy Mayo Roasted Honeynut Squash

In this recipe, Honeynut squash gets the ultimate spicy tuna treatment; it's like a deconstructed roll reconstructed into a cute little squash. If you're new to Honeynut squash, it's a cross between a butternut squash and buttercup squash with supersweet flesh (like honey!) and an edible skin. It's also compact, and I like to think of it as personal-size. Look for deeply orange ones with little to no green striping on the skin or stem. If you can't get your hands on Honeynut squash, don't worry; substitute a couple of acorn squash and plan to roast them for 5 to 10 minutes longer.

Serves 4

4 Honeynut squash

3 tablespoons unsalted butter, melted

3 tablespoons Kewpie mayonnaise

1 tablespoon sriracha

1 teaspoon soy sauce (shoyu)

½ teaspoon toasted sesame oil

For Serving

1 avocado, thinly sliced

Thai sweet chili sauce, for drizzling

Toasted sesame oil, for drizzling

1 green onion, thinly sliced

Furikake

A few sheets of roasted seasoned nori sheets, thinly sliced or torn into small pieces

Cooked rice of your choice

Preheat the oven to 425°F. Line a half-sheet pan with parchment paper.

Cut each squash in half lengthwise and scoop the seeds out with a spoon. Set the halves on the lined sheet pan and evenly drizzle the butter on both sides of the squash, using your hands to coat them. Arrange the halves cut-side down and roast until very soft with caramelized edges on the cut side, 25 to 30 minutes.

Meanwhile, in a small bowl, mix together the mayo, sriracha, soy sauce, and sesame oil.

To serve: Place the roasted squash, cut-side up, on a plate. Fan out avocado slices on top. Drizzle on the spicy mayo. Drizzle on some sweet chili sauce and sesame oil and sprinkle with green onions, furikake, and nori. Serve with your choice of rice. This is a fork-and-knife dish versus a sushi hand-rolling experience.

Dynamite Portobello

Sushi bakes are a Hawai'i thing. Think of them as a big pan of sushi casserole, baked in the oven and served with roasted seasoned nori sheets that you can use to build a handroll. Sushi bakes can have everything, including tuna, mushrooms, water chestnuts, cucumbers, green onions, and always mayo. These baked portobellos are like individual sushi bakes, with the rice on the side!

Serves 4

Everyday Quickle (page 164)

8 portobello mushrooms, cleaned

8 teaspoons extra-virgin olive oil

Kosher salt

3 tablespoons Kewpie mayonnaise

1 tablespoon sriracha

1 teaspoon soy sauce (shoyu)

½ teaspoon toasted sesame oil, plus more for serving

For Serving

1 avocado, diced

Unagi sauce

2 green onions, thinly sliced

Furikake

A few sheets of roasted seasoned nori sheets, thinly sliced or torn into small pieces

Cooked rice of your choice

Preheat the oven to 400°F. Line a half-sheet pan with parchment paper.

Make the quickle as directed and set aside.

Pull off and discard (or save for stock) the portobello stems. Use a spoon to gently scrape off all the gills, starting from the center and pushing out. Lightly score a crosshatch pattern on the tops of all the mushrooms. This helps the steam to vent while they are baking.

Brush each mushroom, top and bottom, with 1 teaspoon of olive oil per mushroom, then sprinkle a small pinch of salt onto each top and bottom.

Arrange on the lined sheet pan, tops up, ensuring the mushrooms aren't touching. Bake for 12 minutes.

Meanwhile, in a small bowl, mix together the mayo, sriracha, soy sauce, and sesame oil.

Flip the mushrooms over (tops down) and brush some spicy mayo onto each mushroom, reserving any extra mayo for serving. Bake for another 6 to 8 minutes.

Place the roasted mushrooms mayo-side up on a plate. Top with a layer of quickles and some avocado. Drizzle with unagi sauce, then sprinkle on green onions, furikake, and nori.

Drizzle the reserved spicy mayo on top. Serve with your choice of rice and any remaining quickles. This is a fork-and-knife dish versus a sushi hand-rolling experience.

Today, most local households have at least one rice cooker, a testament to our great love of rice here on the islands. We love it generously scooped onto a mixed plate lunch. We love it delicately packed into an onigiri or musubi. Fried rice is a favorite of mine, especially when it's a clean-out-the-fridge, don't-want-to-think kind of day. Lately, I have thought, What if we could expand upon this? Jazz it up a bit, maybe add a little flair to celebrate it. Maybe even swap it out for something with a bit more fiber or protein, like farro or quinoa, from time to time. But still honor the staple grain that is rice, just with more flavor, more bite, more variety.

This isn't to say that I don't find myself craving a giant scoop of steamed white rice—because I do, and when I want it, I make it. But this chapter is devoted to the "more is more" philosophy. More options are the goal here. In keeping with the spirit of this book, we are looking at local favorites and expanding upon them. Whether it's spicing up a pot of everyday steamed white rice, turning old rice into something new, or even swapping it out for an entirely new grain, these are some new takes on the classic and beloved rice. This also opens the door to other possibilities outside rice, including locally sourced options like kalo (taro), ʻulu (breadfruit), and ʻuala (sweet potato). Here's a guide to the subchapters in Starches. →

starches

MIXED RICE

These dishes use Hawai'i's favorite steamed white rice as their base and add other ingredients for flavor, heartiness, and texture. Edamame rice is a local favorite and oftentimes served at potlucks.

FRIED RICE

Spam fried rice is a local standby for breakfast, lunch, or dinner—using leftover rice and fridge and pantry staples to create a main dish. Steamed white rice that is stir-fried with veggies, eggs, and various seasonings can beef up any meal.

CRISPY RICE

This is not a traditional dish in local Hawai'i food culture, but it is a great way to repurpose leftover grains and give them new textures and life.

MASH

Reimaging the possibilities of mashed potatoes, this subchapter uses local staples like sweet potatoes ('uala), kabocha squash, taro (kalo), and breadfruit ('ulu) to add new options to a dish most people know and love.

'Ulupalakua, Maui

Mushroomy Rice

This umami-packed mushroomy rice is meant to be served alongside your favorite main, but it's good enough to stand alone—and is great topped with a fried egg. Featuring mushrooms done three ways, it employs minimal extra steps and boasts maximum reward. My husband, Moses, dubbed it one of his favorite recipes and has made it on a regular basis—it's that good! For fresh mushrooms, I recommend using a few, like oyster, king trumpets, and button mushrooms. Nametake is a seasoned enoki mushroom that is both sweet and savory and is usually found in a jar in Asian markets or even the Asian foods aisle at many grocery stores.

Makes 7 cups

5 dried shiitake mushrooms, rinsed and cleaned to remove debris

2½ cups boiling water

2 cups Kokuho Rose or other medium-grain rice

1 teaspoon kosher salt, plus more for seasoning

8 ounces assorted fresh mushrooms, cleaned and trimmed, if necessary

2 tablespoons unsalted butter

Freshly ground black pepper

2 garlic cloves, minced

1 tablespoon soy sauce (shoyu)

3 tablespoons nametake (seasoned enoki mushrooms)

In a heatproof bowl, combine the mushrooms and boiling water and soak for 10 to 15 minutes, until rehydrated. Scoop out the mushrooms and squeeze the excess liquid back into the bowl. Cut off any tough stems, thinly slice the shiitake mushroom caps, and set both the mushrooms and soaking liquid aside.

Add the rice to the pot of a rice cooker and rinse the rice with warm water three times, mixing it with your hand in a repetitive circular motion, counting to ten, allowing some of the starch to release from the grains, and draining each time. Next, add the shiitake soaking liquid to the rice. You should have enough liquid to hit the 2-cup line, but add a little more water if not. Mix in the salt. Add the shiitakes to the top of the rice and cook the rice according to the rice cooker settings.

While the rice is cooking, prepare the fresh mushrooms. Tear them into bite-size pieces or, in the case of king trumpet or button mushrooms, cut into ¼-inch-thick pieces or rounds.

In a large skillet, melt the butter over medium heat. When the butter is gently bubbling, add the mushrooms and season with a big pinch of salt and a few grinds of pepper. Stir to coat the mushrooms evenly, then cook untouched for 5 minutes. Give the mushrooms a quick stir, then add the garlic. Cook until the garlic has softened, another 2 to 3 minutes. Turn off the heat and add the soy sauce, stirring the mushrooms to coat them evenly.

It's time to combine the flavors when the rice is finished cooking. Wait 5 minutes before opening the lid of the rice cooker and fluffing the rice using a rice paddle or spatula. Then, toss in the cooked mushrooms and the nametake enoki. Mix well and serve.

Lapaʻau Farm

Location
Olinda, Maui, Hawaiʻi

Farm Stats
2 acres
3,200-foot elevation

Growing
Various root crops, salad greens, brassicas, alliums, nightshades (like tomatoes and eggplants), cucumbers, oyster mushrooms, and cut flowers

Founded
2018

Owners
Michael and Lauren Marchand

Our most basic farming philosophy is to promote soil health as the foundation of what we do, to grow the most nutrient-rich produce that we can. —Lauren Marchand

I first learned of Lapaʻau Farm through their oyster mushrooms. Harvesting anywhere from four hundred to five hundred pounds of oyster mushrooms per week, Lapaʻau Farm has become a great local source of oyster mushrooms on the island of Maui. They are distributed to local grocery stores, restaurants, and through their CSA (community-supported agriculture). My husband and I have been proud supporters of their CSA for two years and counting, and we look forward to our biweekly deliveries of farm-fresh goodies. The two-acre farm is one of the most beautiful I've seen, every inch of it teeming with life and beauty.

The farm's founders hope to change and evolve local food culture, both in growing more food for local distribution and making locally grown produce more accessible. They run their farm using regenerative agriculture, sharing their hard-earned knowledge with local organizations, such as the Hawaiʻi Farmers Union United, the Maui Nui Food Alliance, and The Common Ground Collective, which brings them closer to their goals. Listening to their CSA members and local chef partners, the Marchands continue to grow and expand their offerings based on community needs. They hope to inspire future local farmers and farms to start their own organic and regenerative farms to feed the people.

Choy Sum Rice

This rice utilizes just a few ingredients, comes together quickly, and allows the clean, green flavor of the choy sum, a tender, long-stemmed, leafy green veggie, to shine. Accented by a generous amount of garlic, this rice pairs with just about anything and can stand alone if you're craving something green. I am a massive fan of the greens you get at a Chinese restaurant. Think of this as restaurant-style Chinese greens meets rice. Because the choy sum is chopped up into bite-size bits, it allows you to skip a few steps, like covering the pan with a lid to steam it, and it shaves off a few minutes because the pieces cook quickly, amounting to a lot less fuss.

Makes 7 cups

2 cups Kokuho Rose or other medium-grain rice

2 teaspoons kosher salt

1 pound choy sum

1 tablespoon neutral oil (see page 18)

5 garlic cloves, finely minced

½ teaspoon cooking wine, such as Shaoxing or sake

½ teaspoon sugar

Add the rice to the pot of a rice cooker and rinse the rice with warm water three times, mixing it with your hand in a repetitive circular motion, counting to ten, allowing some of the starch to release from the grains, and draining each time. Fill the pot with water to the 2-cup line and stir in 1 teaspoon of the salt. Cook the rice according to the rice cooker settings.

While the rice is cooking, prepare the choy sum. Trim the ends of the choy sum until you no longer see any white in the center of the stem. Divide the leaves from the stems and chop both the stems and leaves into ½-inch pieces.

When the rice is finished cooking, wait 5 minutes before opening the lid and fluffing it using a rice paddle or spatula.

In a large skillet, heat the oil over medium heat until it is shiny. Swirl the pan a few times to help distribute the oil, then add the garlic and stir-fry for 30 seconds or until fragrant. Add the choy sum stems and stir-fry until the stems look bright green and shiny, 1 to 2 minutes. Add the leaves and stir-fry for a minute to soften the leaves. Add the cooking wine, sugar, and the remaining 1 teaspoon salt and sauté for 1 more minute. Mix the choy sum into the rice using your rice paddle and serve warm.

Edamame Rice

A hero potluck dish that is just as good any day of the week, edamame rice is a crowd favorite here in Hawai'i. It utilizes four simple ingredients: rice, shelled edamame, ochazuke furikake, and nametake, which do all the heavy lifting, leaving you with a delicious, flavor-packed rice that will surely become a staple in your household. You should be able to find shelled edamame in your grocery store freezer section. Ochazuke furikake is a type of furikake with salted wakame (seaweed) and toasted rice crackers. I find myself serving this mixed rice with scrambled eggs or a few soy-marinated eggs when I can't be bothered to cook.

Makes 7 cups

2 cups Kokuho Rose or other medium-grain rice

1 teaspoon kosher salt

¼ cup ochazuke furikake

¼ cup nametake (seasoned enoki mushrooms)

1 cup shelled edamame, cooked

Add the rice to the pot of a rice cooker and rinse the rice with warm water three times, mixing it with your hand in a repetitive circular motion, counting to ten, allowing some of the starch to release from the grains, and draining each time. Fill the pot with water to the 2-cup line and stir in the salt. Cook the rice according to the rice cooker settings.

When the rice is finished cooking, wait 5 minutes before opening the lid and fluffing it using a rice paddle or spatula. Then fold in the furikake, nametake, and edamame, mix well, and serve.

Azuki Bean Rice

This mixed rice recipe is deeply inspired by sekihan, steamed sticky (sweet) rice with azuki (red) beans. My nontraditional azuki bean rice is made with Calrose rice or short-grain rice in a fraction of the time and is lighter than its dense yet delicious counterpart. Sekihan is a celebratory dish traditionally served for special occasions and often associated with the new year. In Japanese culture, red is considered a lucky color, symbolizing happiness and prosperity. Because this dish is made with sticky rice, it takes time and energy. However, I absolutely love it and think the sweet red azuki beans and salty black sesame seeds pair well with many of my favorite dishes, like Shoyu Kabocha (page 26), Roasted Miso Sweet Potato (page 53), and anything mochiko (pages 90 to 91).

Makes 7 cups

½ cup dried azuki beans

2½ cups water

2 cups Kokuho Rose or other medium-grain rice

1 teaspoon kosher salt

1 tablespoon toasted black sesame seeds

½ teaspoon flaky salt

Rinse the azuki beans in a fine-mesh sieve, then add to a medium saucepan. Add water to cover and bring to a boil over medium-high heat. Once the water comes to a boil, turn off the heat and drain the beans in the fine-mesh sieve.

Return the beans to the saucepan and add the 2½ cups water. Bring it to a boil over medium-high heat. Reduce the heat to low, cover, and simmer until the beans have softened but aren't completely cooked, 40 to 45 minutes. Set the fine-mesh sieve over a bowl and drain the beans. Set the beans in a separate bowl and let them and the cooking liquid cool. This should take about 1 hour.

Once the bean cooking liquid is cooled to room temperature, you can begin cooking the rice. Add the rice to the pot of a rice cooker and rinse the rice with warm water three times, mixing it with your hand in a repetitive circular motion, allowing some of the starch to release from the grains, and draining each time. Add the reserved bean cooking liquid to the rice, adding water as needed to hit the 2-cup line. Mix in the kosher salt. Add the cooked beans to the top of the rice and cook the rice according to the rice cooker settings.

When the rice is done cooking, let it sit for 10 minutes before opening the lid of the rice cooker, then carefully fluff it using a rice paddle or spatula. In a small bowl, mix together the sesame seeds and the flaky salt with your hands, pinching the salt flakes between your fingers to break them into smaller pieces. This mixture is called gomashio.

Sprinkle the gomashio on top of individual servings.

Garlicky Green Bean Fried Rice

We usually make fried rice on the nights we need to clean out the fridge, and because it's often our main dish, it's bursting with flavor. However, fried rice can be a fantastic, quiet side dish that bolsters a main. This fried rice does just that. It's good enough to eat alone or with some fluffy, buttery scrambled eggs, but the flavors are neutral enough to pair with almost anything else, from Daikon Adobo (page 85) to Miso Cabbage (page 49). The beans are meant to keep some of their squeaky crunch to add some textural intrigue to the rice. Keep in mind that I find fried rice turns out best when using day-old, straight-from-the-fridge rice.

Serves 4

2 tablespoons neutral oil (see page 18), plus more as needed

6 garlic cloves, thinly sliced

8 ounces green beans, trimmed and chopped into ½-inch pieces

2 green onions, chopped, green and white parts kept separate

Kosher salt and freshly ground black pepper

3 cups day-old steamed Kokuho Rose or other medium-grain white rice, refrigerated

2 teaspoons soy sauce (shoyu)

1 large egg, beaten

In a wok or large skillet, heat the oil over medium heat until shiny. Add the garlic and sauté until it softens and begins turning golden brown, 1 to 2 minutes. Quickly, before the garlic gets too dark, remove it with a slotted spoon and set aside on a plate.

Add the green beans and the white parts of the green onions, season with salt and pepper, and sauté for a minute or two to kiss the beans with some heat but not overcook them. They should turn bright green. Add the rice, reserved garlic, and soy sauce, mixing and breaking the rice up with your spoon. Stir-fry until the rice is hot and drying out, 5 to 7 minutes. If you see a rice grain pop up from the pan, that's a good sign. Taste and add more salt and pepper as needed.

Push the rice to the edges of the pan to create a well in the middle. If the pan needs it, add some oil to the center well. Pour in the egg and let sit for 30 seconds before scrambling the mixture. Continue scrambling until the egg is cooked, breaking it into small pieces as you go. Incorporate the scrambled egg into the rice and sprinkle in the tops of the green onions. Stir-fry for 1 minute more. Serve in bowls.

Ginger Cabbage Fried Farro

When I was living in Los Angeles, I got used to ancient grains like farro and quinoa being mainstays on most menus. When we moved back home, I started to think about what role ancient grains could play in our everyday menu, which is to say that I questioned how to pair them with local flavors. I am unafraid to admit that I don't love them alone; they need some assistance to make it onto my plate. Farro's chewiness and nuttiness work beautifully in a dish like fried "rice." Stir-frying the farro with sweet ribbons of cabbage and finishing it with frizzled ginger has changed my mind regarding farro. As with my other fried rice recipes, I recommend using day-old farro, straight from the fridge, so plan accordingly!

Serves 4

2 tablespoons neutral oil (see page 18), plus more as needed

3-inch piece fresh ginger, peeled and finely julienned

½ red onion, diced

½ small head green or red cabbage, thinly sliced

2 garlic cloves, minced

3 cups day-old cooked farro, refrigerated

1 tablespoon soy sauce (shoyu)

1 teaspoon rice vinegar

½ teaspoon sugar

½ teaspoon kosher salt

1 large egg, beaten

½ teaspoon toasted sesame oil

1 green onion, thinly sliced, for serving

Black pepper

In a wok or large skillet, heat the neutral oil over medium heat until shiny. Add the ginger and stir-fry until golden brown and crisp, about 3 minutes. Use a slotted spoon to remove it and set aside on a plate. Add the onion and cook until the onion is just translucent and fragrant, about 5 minutes. Add the cabbage and garlic and cook until the cabbage has softened, about 5 minutes.

Add the farro, drizzle on the soy sauce and vinegar, sprinkle on the sugar and salt, and stir-fry until the farro is hot and drying out, 5 to 7 minutes.

Push the farro to the edges of the pan to create a well in the middle. If the pan needs it, add some neutral oil to the center well. Pour the beaten egg in and let sit for 30 seconds before scrambling the mixture. Continue scrambling until the egg is cooked, breaking it into small pieces as you go. Incorporate the scrambled egg into the farro, add the reserved ginger, and stir-fry for 1 minute more. Remove the wok from the heat and drizzle on the sesame oil.

Serve in bowls with green onion and a few cracks of black pepper on top.

Shiitake and Kale Fried Quinoa

If you're like me and find the texture of freshly cooked fluffy quinoa somewhat off-putting, cool it down to room temperature, refrigerate it, and make this fried rice quinoa. In my book, stir-frying is the key to a delicious, earthy grain. I love the shiitake chew and the thin kale whispers throughout the quinoa.

Serves 4

8 dried shiitake mushrooms, rinsed and cleaned to remove debris

2 tablespoons neutral oil (see page 18), plus more as needed

½ sweet onion, diced

½ teaspoon kosher salt

One 8-ounce bunch lacinato (dino) kale, midribs removed and thinly sliced

2 garlic cloves, minced

½-inch piece fresh ginger, peeled and finely grated

3 cups day-old cooked quinoa, refrigerated

1 tablespoon soy sauce (shoyu)

1 tablespoon vegetarian oyster sauce

1 teaspoon rice vinegar

1 large egg, beaten

½ teaspoon toasted sesame oil

Toasted sesame seeds, for serving

Start by soaking the shiitakes for 20 minutes in a bowl with enough hot water to cover them. After 20 minutes, squeeze the excess water from the shiitakes (reserve this shiitake broth for another use like the Hearty Veggie Portuguese Bean Soup on page 64). Cut off any tough stems, thinly slice the shiitake mushroom caps, and set aside.

In a wok or large skillet, heat the neutral oil over medium heat until shiny. Add the onion, sprinkle with kosher salt, and cook until the onion is just translucent and fragrant, about 5 minutes. Add the kale and garlic and cook until the kale has softened, 2 to 3 minutes. Add the ginger and stir-fry until softened and fragrant, 1 to 2 minutes.

Add the quinoa, then drizzle in the soy sauce, oyster sauce, and vinegar, and stir-fry until the quinoa is hot and drying out, 5 to 7 minutes.

Push the quinoa to the edges of the pan to create a well in the middle. If the pan needs it, add some neutral oil to the center well. Pour in the beaten eggs and let sit for 30 seconds before scrambling the mixture. Continue scrambling until the egg is cooked, breaking it into small pieces as you go. Incorporate the scrambled egg into the quinoa and stir-fry for 1 minute more. Remove the wok from the heat and drizzle on the sesame oil.

Serve in bowls with sesame seeds on top.

Kimchi Carrot Fried Rice

Funky and flavorful, kimchi—or kim chee, and no, that's not a typo, but how it's commonly spelled here—rice is the opposite of quiet. This fried rice demands attention, and that's why we love it. The carrot adds an unexpected sweetness that complements the heat, softening the punch of the rice just a touch. The color is so striking that anyone seeing this rice on their plate will light up, recognizing instantly what they're about to eat. Simple and easy to make, this can be turned into a main dish with a few fried eggs.

Serves 4

2 tablespoons neutral oil (see page 18)

1 tablespoon unsalted butter

1 small sweet onion, diced

1½ cups kimchi, roughly chopped

2 carrots, julienned

3 cups day-old steamed Kokuho Rose or other medium-grain white rice, refrigerated

2 teaspoons soy sauce (shoyu)

2 tablespoons kimchi juice

1 tablespoon gochujang (Korean chile paste)

1 teaspoon gochugaru (Korean chile flakes)

Kosher salt

1 tablespoon toasted sesame oil

1 green onion, thinly sliced, for serving

Toasted sesame seeds, for serving

Finely shredded nori (dried seaweed), for serving

In a wok or large skillet, heat the neutral oil and butter over medium heat until the butter has melted. Add the onion and cook until the onion is just translucent and fragrant, about 5 minutes. Add the kimchi and carrots and cook until most of the liquid has cooked off, 4 to 5 minutes.

Add the rice, soy sauce, kimchi juice, gochujang, and gochugaru and stir-fry until the rice is hot and drying out, 5 to 7 minutes. Add more neutral oil if needed. If you see a rice grain pop up from the pan, that's a good sign. Taste and add salt as needed.

Remove the wok from the heat and drizzle on the sesame oil. Give everything a good stir to combine. Serve in bowls with green onions, sesame seeds, and nori on top.

Pan-Seared Crispy Rice

Two kinds of crispy rice make frequent appearances at our table. This is the first type, with the crisp on the outside, on the edges, but still chewy on the inside. A couple of elements make it sing, the first being butter. Please don't skimp on the butter! It adds a creaminess that should not be missed. The other crucial component is toppings! The fried garlic is a must! As with fried rice, this dish works best with day-old rice straight from the fridge. The drier rice is essential for achieving that magic crispiness. You can also serve with your favorite chili crisp oil or Green Onion Oil (page 27). Simply drizzle a few spoonfuls of either before serving.

Serves 4

1 tablespoon unsalted butter

1 tablespoon reserved garlic oil (from fried garlic recipe, below)

3 cups day-old steamed Kokuho Rose or other medium-grain white rice, refrigerated

Kosher salt

Fried Garlic (recipe follows)

In a large skillet, heat the butter and oil over medium-high heat. When the butter has melted, add the rice, spreading it in an even layer and sprinkle with kosher salt. Firmly press the rice with a wooden spoon; it should look a little like a rice pancake. Cook the rice undisturbed until golden and crispy on the bottom, 7 to 10 minutes. You can check to see if it's ready by peeling up an edge and looking underneath. When it's ready, break the "pancake" up into pieces and plate.

Sprinkle the fried garlic atop the crispy rice when serving.

Note: Coconut rice makes excellent crispy rice. To make it, in a rice cooker, start with 2 cups Kokuho Rose rice or another medium-grain rice and substitute half of the water with one 13.5-ounce can full-fat coconut milk.

Fried Garlic

Makes about 2 to 3 tablespoons

6 garlic cloves, minced

3 tablespoons neutral oil (see page 18)

¼ teaspoon kosher salt

Set a fine-mesh sieve over a bowl and set aside. In a small saucepan, combine the garlic and oil and cook over medium-high heat, stirring frequently to ensure none of the garlic is sticking, until the garlic is a light golden brown, 2 to 4 minutes.

Immediately pour the garlic and oil into the sieve. Immediately sprinkle the salt on the crispy garlic. Use 1 tablespoon of the garlic oil when cooking your crispy rice. Sprinkle the garlic atop the crispy rice when serving.

Rice Crispies

This is the second type of crispy rice we eat in our house. I like to think of it as a crispy rice topping. I usually add it to salads for crunch and to make the salad feel more substantial. While the first version is cooked on the stovetop, this second version is baked in the oven. It takes a little longer, but it's very hands-off, and gives you max crisp with minimal effort.

Crispy toppings like crispy rice, crispy quinoa, and crispy farro aren't the first starches you'd think of pairing with local dishes, especially when you're used to picturing it like a plate lunch with a big scoop of white rice on the side of a generous heap of something meaty. However, you're still getting your starch, even if you're sprinkling it on top, and what's more, it's adding value with the textural boost it provides.

Makes 2 cups

2 cups day-old steamed Kokuho Rose or other medium-grain white rice, refrigerated

2 tablespoons extra-virgin olive oil

½ teaspoon kosher salt

¼ to ½ teaspoon freshly ground black pepper

Preheat the oven to 400°F. Line a half-sheet pan with parchment paper.

In a bowl, toss the rice with the olive oil, salt to taste, and pepper. Pour the rice onto the lined sheet pan and arrange in an even layer. Bake until golden and crispy, 30 to 35 minutes, stirring it halfway through.

Let it cool slightly on the sheet pan before serving. Serve on top of your favorite salad.

Variations

Shoyu Rice Crispies

*Substitute **neutral oil** (see page 18) for the olive oil. Omit the salt and pepper. Toss the rice with **2 tablespoons soy sauce** (shoyu), **1 finely grated garlic clove**, **¼-inch piece fresh ginger** (peeled and finely grated), and **½ teaspoon sugar**. Bake as directed.*

Chili Crisp Rice Crispies

*Omit the olive oil and use **1 tablespoon toasted sesame oil** and **1 tablespoon chili crisp oil**. Omit the salt and pepper. Stir **1 tablespoon soy sauce** (shoyu) into the rice and bake as directed.*

Garlic Rice Crispies

*Substitute **neutral oil** (see page 18) for the olive oil. Omit the pepper. Stir **2 finely grated garlic cloves** and **1 teaspoon garlic powder** into the rice. Bake as directed.*

Quinoa Crispies

While you can make crispy quinoa in the oven, it's much faster to cook it on the stovetop, and I find that you get a more even crisp when you do so. Note that, unlike the other crispies, you don't need to refrigerate the quinoa, only cool it to room temperature. Serve atop a salad or a main dish like Huli Huli Zucchini (page 41) instead of the crispy chickpeas.

Makes 2 cups

2 tablespoons extra-virgin olive oil

2 cups cooked quinoa, cooled

½ teaspoon kosher salt

In a large skillet, heat the olive oil over medium heat until shiny. Add the quinoa and spread into a thin layer. Cook, stirring occasionally, until golden brown and crispy, 15 to 18 minutes. When the quinoa starts vigorously popping in the pan, you'll know you're close. Sprinkle on the salt, stirring, and remove the pan from the heat. Let the quinoa cool completely before serving.

Farro Crispies

Farro is an excellent candidate for crispiness because its chewy nuttiness is enhanced when it's broiled. Crispy farro adds wonderful texture to salads and mains alike, and while cooked farro is a great base in grain bowls, it's just as exciting as a crispy topper. Serve atop a salad or a main dish like Shoyu-Roasted Carrots (page 29).

Makes 2 cups

2 cups day-old cooked farro, refrigerated

2 tablespoons extra-virgin olive oil

½ teaspoon kosher salt

Set an oven rack 5 inches below the heating element and then turn the broiler on high.

In a bowl, toss the farro with the olive oil and salt and spread it evenly on a half-sheet pan. Broil for 2 minutes. Remove the pan to stir the farro well, spread it into an even layer again, and broil for 3 to 5 minutes. Watch the farro closely; don't walk away, the farro can go from perfectly crispy to burnt quickly. It's done when the farro is lightly toasted.

Remove it from the oven and let it cool on the sheet pan for 10 minutes. It will continue to crisp as it cools.

Coconut Sweet Potato Mash

This simple mashed Okinawan sweet potato dish presents as fussier than it is. It is the most beautiful, rich purple color thanks to the potatoes, and it is scented with coconut and sweetness. Because the potatoes are roasted for a long time, they take on a note of brown sugar that gives off big caramel vibes when combined with coconut milk and butter. It's so good you'll be lucky if it makes it onto your plate; we've been guilty of eating it by the spoonful straight out of the bowl.

Serves 4 to 6

2 pounds Okinawan sweet potatoes, scrubbed and patted dry

½ cup canned full-fat coconut milk

4 tablespoons unsalted butter

½ teaspoon kosher salt, plus more as needed

Preheat the oven to 425°F. Line a half-sheet pan with parchment paper.

Using a fork, poke holes all over the sweet potatoes, aiming to prick each sweet potato at least 5 times. Arrange the potatoes on the lined sheet pan, ensuring none of the potatoes are touching. Roast the potatoes until the flesh starts collapsing in the skin, 45 minutes to 1 hour 15 minutes, depending on the size of your potatoes. Start checking for doneness at the 45-minute mark. They're done when it feels like the skin is pulling away from the flesh when you gently press it with an oven mitt–fitted hand.

Let the potatoes sit on the sheet pan until they're cool enough to touch. Halve the potatoes lengthwise and scoop the flesh into a bowl with a spoon.

In a small saucepan, heat the coconut milk and butter over medium-low heat until the butter has melted and the mixture is hot. (Alternatively, heat in a bowl in the microwave in 30-second intervals.)

Pour half of the mixture over the potatoes and use a potato masher or wooden spoon to gently incorporate the liquid into the potatoes while you're lightly mashing. Mash until well combined and creamy but with some potato chunks. Season with the salt, adding more to taste if desired. Serve immediately, finishing it with a drizzle of the remaining coconut mixture.

Kabocha Mash

If you want to grow a lot of something, start a few kabocha plants. In the blink of an eye, you'll be swimming in kabocha squash! And if you're anything like me, that's a problem you'd like to have. Sweet and, dare I say, chestnut-like, kabocha tends to be denser than other winter squash and creamier when roasted. It makes a luxurious mash that is a great starch for any dish.

Serves 4 to 6

1 small kabocha squash (2 pounds)

1 tablespoon extra-virgin olive oil

½ cup whole milk

½ cup vegetable broth

4 tablespoons unsalted butter (2 ounces/½ stick)

½ teaspoon kosher salt, plus more as needed

Chili crisp oil, for serving

2 green onions, chopped, for serving

Preheat the oven to 425°F. Line a quarter-sheet pan with parchment paper.

Cut the kabocha in half first by removing the stem and making small cuts around the stem with the heel of your knife. Once you've made your way around the stem, do the same again, but use the tip of your knife to cut deeper. Repeat this process on the bottom of the squash. Use a rocking motion rather than trying to use brute force to cut the squash in half. Scoop the seeds out using a spoon.

Rub the flesh of the kabocha with the olive oil and place cut-side down on the lined sheet pan. Roast until the flesh is tender enough to be easily pierced with a knife, 35 to 40 minutes. The cut side should be caramelized.

Let it cool until it's cool enough to touch. Scoop the flesh into a bowl.

In a small saucepan, heat the milk, broth, and butter together over medium-low heat until the butter has melted and the mixture is hot. (Alternatively, heat in a bowl in the microwave in 30-second intervals.) Pour half of the milk mixture over the kabocha and lightly mash with a potato masher or wooden spoon to gently incorporate the liquid into the squash while you're lightly mashing. Mash until well combined and creamy but with some kabocha chunks. Add more liquid as needed; this will be determined by how much moisture is in your kabocha. Season with the salt, adding more to taste if desired. Serve immediately, topped with chili crisp oil and green onions.

Taro Mash

This nutty, chewy taro (kalo) mash is closer to a chunky mashed potato than to poi, a staple food in Hawai'i that is a smooth paste made with steamed taro. This taro mash is a side I dreamed up one night when I thought of flavors I love. With flavors akin to a taro poke—a dish that consists of steamed cubed taro tossed in a mixture of Hawaiian salt ('alaea), soy sauce (shoyu), sesame oil, and some onions—this mash is highly craveable. To clean your taro, wash and scrub it, trimming any long roots by snapping them off by hand or with a paring knife. Uncooked taro has calcium oxalate, so I recommend you wear gloves when handling it raw, as your hands might get a little itchy without them. I highly recommend serving this with laulau (see page 58) and some Shoyu Onion Quickle (page 167).

Serves 4 to 6

2 pounds taro (kalo), cleaned

¼ sweet onion, small diced

2 green onions, chopped

½-inch piece fresh ginger, peeled and finely grated

1 garlic clove, finely grated

2 tablespoons soy sauce (shoyu)

1 tablespoon toasted sesame oil

¾ teaspoon Hawaiian salt ('alaea)

Set a steamer basket over a large pot or pan filled with water to a height of 3 to 4 inches. Bring the water to a boil over medium-high heat, then promptly reduce the heat to medium-low to keep at a steady simmer. Set the taro in the basket and replace the lid. Steam until it's very tender and easily pierced with a knife, 2 to 3 hours.

When it's cool enough to touch but still warm, peel and remove all the skin. Cut the taro into ½-inch cubes and place in a bowl. To the bowl, add the onion, green onions, ginger, garlic, soy sauce, sesame oil, and Hawaiian salt. Toss to coat the taro evenly. Give everything a gentle mash using a potato masher or wooden spoon, barely mashing everything together. Be careful not to overmash; the mixture will become stickier the more you mash it. It's best scooped with a disher or big ice cream scoop. Serve immediately.

Note: This dish is equally good cold and can double as a mayo-less taro salad. It can also be fried like a hash and served with a fried egg.

Garlicky Breadfruit Mash

My husband and I tried to grow breadfruit (ʻulu), but our elevation is slightly over 3,000 feet. ʻUlu trees are impressive to behold, vast and majestic, and their leaves are stunning. They can produce hundreds of pounds of fruit annually and do best below 1,500 feet. Our friends at Nohoʻana Farm told us that even if the tree took root, it likely would never fruit. One bite of this mash, adapted from *Sam Choy's ʻUlu Cookbook*, will have you questioning whether you can grow ʻulu. Grab a copy of the book if you ever want to know what to do with ʻulu; it's got a recipe for just about any kind of breadfruit dish you can think of: soups, mains, sides, desserts, and condiments! This mash is garlicky to the max and pairs well with any dish you might pair mashed potatoes with.

Serves 4 to 6

Fried Garlic (page 148)

1 head garlic, top chopped off

1 teaspoon extra-virgin olive oil

Kosher salt

One 2-pound mature breadfruit (ʻulu), peeled and cut into quarters

½ cup half-and-half

3 tablespoons unsalted butter

Preheat the oven to 400°F.

Make the fried garlic as directed and set aside.

Set the head of garlic on a small piece of foil, pour the olive oil over the exposed cloves, and sprinkle with a pinch of salt. Wrap the foil tightly around the head of garlic. Roast, either directly on a rack or placed on a quarter-sheet pan, for 40 minutes. Remove from the oven and let the garlic cool in the foil until ready to use.

Steam the breadfruit (see Note) and, when it is cool enough to touch but still warm, cut it into 1-inch pieces and place in a bowl. Squeeze the cloves from the head of garlic into the bowl.

In a small saucepan, heat the half-and-half and butter over medium-low heat until the butter has melted and the mixture is hot. (Alternatively, heat in a bowl in the microwave in 30-second intervals.) Pour over the breadfruit and lightly mash with a potato masher or wooden spoon to gently incorporate the liquid into the breadfruit while you're mashing. Be careful not to overmash; the mixture will become stickier the more you mash it. Mash until combined and the desired texture has been reached. Season with salt to taste. Top with fried garlic and a drizzle of garlic oil, and serve immediately.

Note: To steam breadfruit, set a steamer basket over a large pot or pan filled with water to a height of 2 inches. Bring the water to a boil over medium-high heat, then promptly reduce the heat to medium-low to keep at a steady simmer. Set the breadfruit in the basket and replace the lid. Steam until tender and easily pierced with a knife, 20 to 30 minutes.

In the equation Main + Starch + Side = Complete Meal, you might feel like skipping over a side to pursue a quicker meal prep situation. However, I encourage you to take a closer look at these recipes. Many of these dishes come together ridiculously fast: See Everyday Quickle (page 164), Tofu Watercress Salad (page 169), or Tomato Poke (page 190). And while some take a little more time, the flavor payoff alone is worth the extra effort. You'll never be disappointed eating that one extra dish that rounds out the plate.

In many ways, these sides represent how lots of meals play out here in Hawai'i. You have a bit of everything and pull it together on one mixed plate, a pūpū (appetizer) party. Let the book's guiding equation be just that, a guide. I fully support you if you want to go another route and build your meal around a couple of sides and maybe something crispy from the Starches chapter. Here is a guide to navigating the subchapters in Sides. →

QUICKLE

These quickles (aka quick pickles) are faster versions of some local favorites, along with my everyday quickle.

SALAD

The salads are built around one master salad dressing for one of Hawai'i's favorite salads, Tofu Watercress (page 169).

POTATO MAC SALAD

In Hawai'i, most plate lunches are built with a good mac or potato mac salad. This subchapter is devoted to a few reimaginings of this classic side.

POKE

The poke subchapter embraces the English translation of *poke*: "to section" or "to slice or cut." Perhaps a little out of the box, these interpretations are bound to delight.

ʻUlupalakua, Maui

Everyday Quickle

This is not a traditional pickle, which is precisely why I love it. There's a time and place for locally loved pickles like takuan, a bright yellow daikon pickle that's tangy and sweet, or pickled onions with ogo, a type of seaweed (limu). However, they take time to pickle, and let's face it, time is of the essence in my house. If there's one veggie that I always try to have on hand, it's cucumber. Crunchy and super hydrating, cucumber is the perfect veg for a quickle, aka quick-pickle. I first learned about quick pickles from Momofuku years ago, but over time, I've tinkered with the ingredients to make them just how I like them. They have become a staple in our house, a little sweet, a little salty, with a note of nuttiness. With just a splash of vinegar, you might hesitate to call them pickles, but these quickles are all about that crisp crunch, not fermentation funk.

Serves 4

2 Japanese cucumbers, thinly sliced

2 teaspoons sugar

1 teaspoon kosher salt

1 teaspoon soy sauce (shoyu)

½ teaspoon rice vinegar

½ teaspoon toasted sesame oil

In a bowl, toss together the cucumbers, sugar, and salt to evenly coat using your hands or a wooden spoon. Let sit for 5 minutes, then add the soy sauce, vinegar, and sesame oil and toss again. Serve immediately or let sit for up to 2 hours.

Quick Kimchi Zucchini

Kimchi (kim chee) is one of my favorite sides for everything from Green Bean Jun (page 95) to Shoyu Cauliflower (page 25). The tangy heat is a welcome addition to most plates. While napa cabbage kimchi is the most well known, I love the versatility of this dish and the fact that there are hundreds of different types of kimchi. This kimchi zucchini can be served the day it's made because it doesn't go thorugh lacto-fermentation. It's fresher in flavor but still just as good.

Serves 4

3 small or 1 large zucchini

1 tablespoon Hawaiian salt ('alaea)

1 tablespoon rice vinegar

2 teaspoons toasted sesame oil

1 tablespoon gochugaru (Korean chile flakes)

¼ teaspoon gochujang (Korean chile paste)

1 teaspoon sugar

1 garlic clove, finely grated

¼ sweet onion, thinly sliced

1 green onion, chopped

Cut off the stem(s) of the zucchini. For small zucchini, cut into ¼-inch-thick rounds. For large zucchini, halve lengthwise and cut crosswise into ¼-inch-thick half-moons. In a bowl, toss the zucchini with the Hawaiian salt and let it sit for 30 minutes. The zucchini should soften and expel lots of moisture.

Rinse it with cold water and drain it in a colander before placing it in a clean kitchen towel, twisting it, and squeezing out the liquid. Rinse and dry the bowl.

In the bowl, combine the vinegar, sesame oil, gochugaru, gochujang, sugar, and garlic and whisk to combine. Add the zucchini, sweet onion, and green onion and toss to combine with your hands or a wooden spoon. Serve immediately or store the kimchi in an airtight container in the refrigerator until you're ready to serve it.

Quick Namasu

It's weird to think of one's dad when thinking of a side dish, but I always think of my dad when I think of namasu. Namasu is essentially thinly sliced vegetables, and sometimes seafood or seaweed, dressed in a bit of vinegar. He loves this dish and makes his version of it often. I'm unsure whether it's the combination of a few veggies or the sweet pickling mixture, but he's a fan. Like most pickles, it usually requires a resting and chilling period, but this quick mix is ready to go as soon as you are done making it.

Serves 4

1 small daikon, peeled and julienned

1 carrot, peeled and julienned

2 Persian (mini) cucumbers, julienned

1½ teaspoons kosher salt

4 teaspoons sugar

3 tablespoons rice vinegar

1 tablespoon water

In a bowl, toss together the daikon, carrot, cucumbers, ½ teaspoon of the salt, and 1 teaspoon of the sugar. Let it sit for 10 minutes.

In a small saucepan, combine the vinegar, water, and the remaining 1 teaspoon salt and 3 teaspoons sugar. Stir over medium heat until the salt and sugar have dissolved. Set aside for 5 minutes.

Pour the pickling mixture over the vegetables and stir to combine. Serve immediately.

Shoyu Onion Quickle

This quickle crosses two of my favorite pickles: shoyu daikon and pickled onions. Thin onion slices are quickly but gently pickled in a mix of a few pantry staples, leaving you with pickles on demand! Great with Potato Cake Katsu with Curry (page 34) or your favorite laulau (see page 58), they're so good you might find yourself snacking on them throughout the day.

Serves 4

¼ cup soy sauce (shoyu)

2 tablespoons rice vinegar

1½ teaspoons sugar

¾ teaspoon kosher salt

1 sweet onion, thinly sliced

½ Hawaiian chile (nīoi) or Thai bird's eye-chile (optional), thinly sliced

In a small saucepan, combine the soy sauce, vinegar, sugar, and salt and cook over medium heat until the sugar and salt have dissolved.

Place the onion and chili pepper (if using) in a small heatproof bowl or jar, then pour the shoyu pickling mixture over. Stir to combine or cover and give it a quick shake. Let the onion "pickle" for 15 to 20 minutes before serving.

Tofu Watercress Salad

For me, this salad is iconic. It is not quite the potluck-style tofu watercress salad, but it brings me back to my teens when my mom and I would pick up a deli container of watercress salad from the grocery store in town. I like to think of it as grocery store watercress salad. The potluck version usually has taegu (spicy dried cod or cuttlefish), whereas the grocery store salad is all about the veggies. Watercress is often overlooked because it's sometimes perceived as bitter or too peppery, but I find that when it's picked at the right time, it's craveable. Fresh and crisp, watercress is ideal for a salad, stir-fry, or soup. This salad hits all the right notes with watercress, tofu, a bright gingery dressing, cherry tomatoes, and cucumber.

Serves 4 to 6

One 16-ounce block firm tofu, drained

2 cups boiling water

2 tablespoons kosher salt

One 1-pound bunch watercress, ends trimmed

1 teaspoon distilled white vinegar

3 tablespoons soy sauce (shoyu)

3 tablespoons rice vinegar

1 teaspoon honey

2 teaspoons sugar

¼-inch piece fresh ginger, peeled and finely grated

1 garlic clove, finely grated

⅛ teaspoon white miso (optional)

1 tablespoon toasted sesame seeds, ground

3 tablespoons neutral oil (see page 18)

2 teaspoons toasted sesame oil

12 ounces cherry tomatoes, quartered

4 ounces bean sprouts

Cut the tofu into 1-inch cubes. In a heatproof bowl, combine the boiling water, salt, and tofu. Let it sit for 10 minutes, then drain and pat the tofu dry with a clean kitchen towel or paper towels. Dry the bowl and return the tofu to the bowl.

Soak the watercress in a large bowl of cold water with the white vinegar for 5 to 10 minutes. This ensures the watercress is as clean as possible and rehydrates the leaves. Drain and rinse thoroughly. Clean and dry the bowl. Spin dry the watercress in a salad spinner; you want it to be as dry as possible. Cut it into 2-inch lengths and place it back into the large bowl.

Meanwhile, in a small bowl, whisk together the soy sauce, rice vinegar, honey, sugar, ginger, garlic, and miso (if using) until the sugar has dissolved. Add the sesame seeds and whisk to combine. Stream in the neutral oil and sesame oil and whisk to emulsify. Set the dressing aside.

To the large bowl with the watercress, add the tofu, tomatoes, and bean sprouts. Pour on the dressing right before serving for the crispest watercress. (Alternatively, you can marinate the tomatoes and tofu in the dressing in a separate bowl and pour it all over the watercress and bean sprouts before serving.)

Shaved Brussels Sprout and Cabbage Salad

Every fall, right before Thanksgiving, Brussels sprouts hit all the grocery store shelves, and I grab a bag, hoping to find a new favorite way to prepare them. I always fall back on shaving them into delicate ribbons and roasting them until they're super crispy. There's a reason I fall back on this method: It delivers. This salad folds those crisp, earthy sprouts into sweet, crunchy cabbage and slightly peppery, juicy daikon, and the salty, sweet, and bright dressing beautifully unifies the flavors.

Serves 4

- 1 pound Brussels sprouts
- 2 tablespoons extra-virgin olive oil
- ½ teaspoon kosher salt
- Shoyu Sesame Dressing (recipe follows)
- ½ small head green cabbage, thinly sliced
- ½ daikon or 1 watermelon radish, thinly sliced

Preheat the oven to 425°F. Line a half-sheet pan with parchment paper.

Trim the stem ends of the Brussels sprouts and remove any outer leaves that look bruised or damaged. Cut each sprout in half through the root end, then thinly slice the halves, creating thin ribbon-like shreds. Place the Brussels sprouts in a bowl and toss with the olive oil and salt. Pour the Brussels sprouts onto the lined sheet pan and arrange them in an even layer.

Roast until golden brown and crispy, about 20 minutes, stirring halfway through. Let the Brussels sprouts cool for 5 to 10 minutes on the sheet pan.

While the Brussels sprouts are roasting, make the dressing as directed.

In a large bowl, combine the cabbage, Brussels sprouts, and daikon radish and dress with half of the dressing. Add more dressing, if desired, to taste and serve immediately.

Shoyu Sesame Dressing

Makes about ½ cup

- 2 tablespoons soy sauce (shoyu)
- 2 tablespoons rice vinegar
- ¾ teaspoon honey
- 1½ teaspoons sugar
- ⅛-inch piece fresh ginger, peeled and finely grated
- ½ garlic clove, finely grated
- ⅛ teaspoon white miso (optional)
- 2 teaspoons toasted sesame seeds, ground
- 3 tablespoons neutral oil (see page 18)
- 1½ teaspoons toasted sesame oil

In a small bowl, whisk together the soy sauce, vinegar, honey, sugar, ginger, garlic, and miso (if using) until the sugar has dissolved. Whisk in the sesame seeds. Stream in the neutral oil and sesame oil and whisk to emulsify.

Kale and Shoyu Mushroom Salad

Years ago, I fell in love with the oyster mushroom tacos in Ottolenghi's *Flavor* and have been putting a Hawai'i twist on them ever since. The mushrooms in this salad are tossed with a flavorful, sweet soy mixture that has strong shoyu chicken vibes; they're roasted at a high heat, delivering many textures at once, which Ottolenghi deftly describes as "crispy, chewy, and soft."

Serves 4 to 6

Shoyu Mushrooms (recipe follows)

Shoyu Sesame Dressing (page 170)

Two 8-ounce bunches lacinato (dino) kale, midribs removed and thinly sliced

2 Persian (mini) cucumbers, thinly sliced on a bias

2 green onions, chopped

Make the shoyu mushrooms as directed.

While the mushrooms are roasting, make the dressing.

In a salad bowl, combine the kale with 1 tablespoon of the dressing. Massage the leaves with the dressing for a minute. Add the cucumbers and green onions and toss with half the dressing. Add more dressing to taste.

Top with the shoyu mushrooms and serve immediately.

Shoyu Mushrooms

I find myself making these Hawai'i-style shoyu mushrooms to add to everything from the above salad to jook (rice porridge) and Coconut Sweet Potato Mash (page 153).

Serves 4 to 6

3 tablespoons neutral oil (see page 18)

3 tablespoons soy sauce (shoyu)

1½ tablespoons maple syrup

2 garlic cloves, finely grated

⅛-inch piece fresh ginger, peeled and finely grated

12 ounces oyster mushrooms, torn into bite-size pieces

Preheat the oven to 425°F. Line a half-sheet pan with parchment paper.

In a medium bowl, whisk together the oil, soy sauce, maple syrup, garlic, and ginger. Toss in the mushrooms and mix well to evenly coat. Pour onto the lined sheet pan and arrange in an even layer, aiming to have no mushrooms touch if possible.

Roast until crispy, 25 to 30 minutes. Let cool on the sheet pan for 5 minutes.

Corn and Avocado Salad

Every summer deserves a corn salad. It screams picnic or beach day. If you're taking it on the go, wait to dress the salad until you reach your destination. I love it paired with Huli Huli Hasselback Butternut Squash (page 46). I just throw some squash on the salad, add some Quinoa Crispies (page 150), and call it a giant summer salad.

Serves 4 to 6

Ginger Lime Candied Peanuts

½ cup unsalted roasted peanuts

1 tablespoon light corn syrup

¼-inch piece fresh ginger, peeled and finely grated

Grated zest of 1 lime

⅛ teaspoon kosher salt

Salad

4 ears corn, husked

Shoyu Sesame Dressing (page 170)

1 Japanese cucumber

1 large or 2 small avocados, cut into 1-inch pieces

2 tablespoons fresh lime juice

Flaky salt, for finishing

To make the ginger lime candied peanuts: Preheat the oven to 350°F. Line a quarter-sheet pan with parchment paper.

In a small bowl, stir together the peanuts, corn syrup, ginger, lime zest, and kosher salt until the peanuts are evenly coated. Pour the peanuts onto the lined sheet pan and spread into an even layer.

Bake until the nuts are golden brown and the coating has thickened, 12 to 15 minutes, stirring halfway through baking. Remove from the oven and let them cool on the baking sheet. Give them a coarse chop when they've cooled.

To make the salad: Preheat an outdoor grill or grill pan to medium-high heat. If you're using a grill pan, set it over medium-high heat and heat for 5 minutes.

Place the corn directly on the grill and cook until all sides are lightly charred, 10 to 12 minutes, turning it every 3 to 4 minutes. Set the corn on a cutting board and let it sit until it's cool enough to touch. Cut the corn kernels from the cob and set in a bowl.

While the corn is cooling, make the dressing and set aside.

Set the cucumber on a cutting board, lay your kitchen knife flat on top of the cucumber, and lightly smash it with your other hand. Roughly chop the smashed sections. Add the cucumber to the bowl. Then add the avocado and dress with half of the dressing, tossing to combine. Evenly drizzle on the lime juice and sprinkle with a couple pinches of flaky salt. Taste, adding more dressing as desired, and sprinkle the peanuts on top. Serve immediately.

Namasu Sweet Potato Salad

One day, when I was eating a plate with some steamed sweet potatoes ('uala) and namasu, a Japanese pickle made with thinly sliced vegetables, I thought, These would be really good together. Now and then, a simple meal can lead to a new way of looking at something you haven't thought twice about in your whole life. There's nothing earth-shattering about a namasu sweet potato salad per se, but one bite, and you'll see what I'm excited about. The pickled veggies really do a lot visually, but it's the combination of the creamy sweet potato and the acidic, crunchy pickles that really works. Creamy and comforting while also punchy and bright.

Serves 4

2 tablespoons kosher salt, plus more as needed

1 pound Okinawan sweet potatoes, peeled

½ cup Quick Namasu (page 166) or store-bought namasu, pickling liquid gently pressed out

2 green onions, chopped, plus more for garnish

½ cup Kewpie mayonnaise, plus more as needed

Freshly ground black pepper

Bring a large pot of water to a boil over high heat. Add the salt and sweet potatoes. Reduce the heat to medium and simmer until a knife can easily pierce the center of a potato, about 30 minutes. Drain and let cool on a cutting board to room temperature. Cut into ½-inch cubes and place in a bowl.

Coarsely chop the namasu and add it to the bowl. Add the green onions and toss until everything is well distributed. Add ¼ cup of the mayo to the bowl and toss until everything is well coated. Taste and season with more salt and pepper. Chill for at least 1 hour before serving. Mix in the remaining ¼ cup of mayo, adding more if you want it creamier, and serve chilled, garnished with green onion.

Breadfruit Mac Salad

If you are a fan of the potato mac salad in *Aloha Kitchen* and find yourself with some breadfruit ('ulu), try this version. Steamed mature breadfruit tastes a lot like a potato, but it's just a little better (IMO) with notes of baked bread and this indescribable greenness I love. Leaning into the green, I've added parsley and celery, but you can always stick to the classic pairing of grated carrots. If you want to add a little more acidity, sweet pickle relish is as good in this breadfruit mac as in the classic potato mac.

Serves 6 to 8

Half a 2-pound mature breadfruit ('ulu), peeled and cut into quarters

Kosher salt

6 ounces ditalini pasta

3 large hard-boiled eggs, peeled and coarsely chopped

1 celery stalk, small diced

3 tablespoons chopped fresh Italian parsley

2 tablespoons grated sweet onion (about ¼ onion)

1¼ cups Kewpie mayonnaise, plus more as needed

1 tablespoon rice vinegar

1 teaspoon sugar

Freshly ground black pepper

Set a steamer basket over a large pot or pan filled with water to a height of 2 inches. Bring the water to a boil over medium-high heat, then promptly reduce the heat to medium-low to keep at a steady simmer. Set the breadfruit in the basket and replace the lid. Steam until tender and easily pierced with a knife, about 20 minutes. When it's cool enough to touch but still warm, cut the breadfruit into ½-inch pieces and place in a bowl.

Meanwhile, bring a pot of salted water to a boil and cook the pasta according to the package directions, but until it is very tender, not al dente.

Drain the pasta, add to the bowl with the breadfruit, and toss together. Let cool for 10 minutes.

Add the eggs, celery, parsley, onion, ¾ cup of the mayo, the vinegar, and sugar. Mix until everything is well coated. Taste and season with salt and pepper. Chill for at least 1 hour before serving.

When you're ready to serve, stir in the remaining ½ cup mayo, adding more if you want it creamier. Serve immediately.

Noho'ana Farm

Location
Waikapū, Maui, Hawai'i

Farm Stats
2 acres
511-foot elevation

Growing
Kalo (taro), 'ulu (breadfruit), mai'a (banana), niu (coconut), kukui (candlenut)

Founded
2004

Owner/Managers
Hōkūao Pellegrino and Alana Ka'ōpūiki-Pellegrino

Our nu'ukia (mission) is: i Ka ho'ōla 'ana i ka 'ike 'ono kupuna ma o ka mahi 'ai ku'una (to revitalize ancestral palates through Hawaiian agricultural practices). The impetus behind restoring Noho'ana was simple yet complex. We love and respect the traditional practices of our ancestral farmers and strongly believe in revitalizing this lifestyle and ensuring the collective region (Nā Wai 'Ehā) gets restored. —Hōkūao Pellegrino

Maui is a small island, so I met Alana Ka'ōpūiki-Pellegrino years ago when we were still in high school. I've admired the work she and her husband, Hōkūao, have been doing to restore their ancestral kuleana (responsibility) land in the ahupua'a (a traditional Hawaiian land division) of Waikapū. It's been a remarkable journey to behold, watching them restore the pā pōhaku kīpapa (stone terraces), lo'i kalo (irrigated terraces for the taro production), and 'auwai (irrigation system) to their original state. They have nurtured their 'ulu agroforestry system and now have twenty-one trees. That may not sound like a lot, unless you're familiar with the 'ulu tree, as each tree can produce hundreds of pounds of fruit annually. The Pellegrinos have strongly advocated restoring water rights to Nā Wai 'Ehā (The Four Waters), consisting of Waikapū, Wailuku, Waiehu, and Waihe'e. What struck me about this farm was how quickly they acted to feed the Lahaina fire victims, providing locally sourced farm-to-table meals weekly for an entire year after the devastation.

The Pellegrinos are integrating endemic Waikapū native plant species to ensure the native ecosystems thrive. In doing so, they hope to restore the land to a state that it would have been in during the time of their ancestors. They hope to see the cultivation of superfoods like 'ulu, kalo, and 'uala expand, as these three crops should be at the forefront of Hawai'i's food sovereignty movement. I asked Hōkūao if there was anything he wanted to share about how to cook with these three crops, and he said, "Whatever you can do with a potato, you can do better with 'ulu, kalo, and 'uala."

Kabocha Potato Salad

This is closer to a Japanese-style potato salad than a Hawai'i-style potato mac salad. It is creamier and somewhere in between a potato salad and mashed potatoes. That being said, it still fills the same hole on your plate. Make it when you're craving something cold and creamy but not quite in the mood for a mac or potato mac salad. It's so good, you may want to double the recipe.

Serves 4

8-ounce wedge kabocha squash, peeled and cut into 1-inch pieces

8 ounces russet potatoes, peeled and cut into 1-inch cubes

1 large hard-boiled egg, peeled and coarsely chopped

¼ cup Kewpie mayonnaise, plus more as needed

1 tablespoon rice vinegar

Kosher salt and freshly ground black pepper

Set a steamer basket over a large pot or pan filled with water to a height of 2 inches. Bring the water to a boil over medium-high heat, then promptly reduce the heat to medium-low to keep at a steady simmer. Set the kabocha and potatoes in the basket and replace the lid. Steam until tender and easily pierced with a knife, 13 to 18 minutes. Transfer the kabocha and potatoes to a bowl and let cool for 10 minutes.

Add the egg, mayo, and vinegar and mix with a wooden spoon, gently mashing some of the pieces as you mix. You want to keep about half of the pieces intact. Add salt and pepper to taste and add more mayo if you want it creamier. Serve warm or chilled if you prefer, chilling for at least 1 hour.

Kimchi Taro Mac Salad

Because one or even two "potato" mac salads aren't enough, here's another, this time with kimchi and taro (kalo). I love using taro in a "potato" mac salad because it adds a chewiness that just works. Everything adheres to the kalo chunks just a little bit better. The kimchi adds a familiar tang, a little heat, and a lot of flavor, replacing the usual vinegar in this dish.

Serves 6

Half a 2-pound taro (kalo)

Kosher salt

8 ounces elbow macaroni

⅓ cup kimchi, diced

2 green onions, chopped

1¼ cups Kewpie mayonnaise, plus more as needed

1 tablespoon kimchi juice

2 teaspoons sugar

Freshly ground black pepper

Set a steamer basket over a large pot or pan filled with water to a height of 3 to 4 inches. Bring the water to a boil over medium-high heat, then promptly reduce the heat to medium-low to keep at a steady simmer. Set the taro in the basket and replace the lid. Steam until it's very tender and easily pierced with a knife, 2 to 3 hours. When it's cool enough to touch but still warm, peel and remove all the skin. Cut the taro into ½-inch cubes and place in a bowl.

Meanwhile, bring a pot of salted water to a boil and cook the pasta according to the package directions, but until it is very tender, not al dente.

Drain the macaroni, add to the bowl with the taro, and toss together. Let cool for 10 minutes.

Add the kimchi, green onions, ¾ cup of the mayo, the kimchi juice, and sugar. Mix until everything is well coated. Taste and season with salt and pepper. Chill for at least 1 hour before serving.

When you're ready to serve, stir in the remaining ½ cup mayo, adding more if you want it creamier. Serve immediately.

Tofu Poke

"To section" or "to slice or cut": This is the English translation of *poke*. While most commonly associated with ruby red cubes of fresh ʻahi (tuna), it's normal to see many interpretations of this dish in local grocers, restaurants, and homes throughout the islands. Rainbows of colors fill the poke cases in Foodland, a large grocery chain in Hawaiʻi. My favorite way to prepare poke at home is using a block of firm tofu. I almost always have it in the fridge, and the tofu really lends itself to the flavors of a classic poke. I find the extra step of quickly brining the block goes a long way in seasoning the tofu and expelling excess liquid (I know this feels counterintuitive, but it does!) and isn't a step to be skipped. Crispy sticks of your favorite root veg add a nice crunch to the dish, and this is where you can get creative with your choice of veggies.

Serves 4

One 16-ounce block firm tofu, drained

2 cups boiling water

2 tablespoons kosher salt

1½ tablespoons soy sauce (shoyu), plus more as needed

1 tablespoon toasted sesame oil

½ teaspoon Hawaiian salt (ʻalaea), plus more as needed

¼ cup thinly sliced red onion

⅓ cup chopped green onions, green tops only

¼ teaspoon gochugaru (Korean chile flakes)

1 tablespoon finely chopped toasted macadamia nuts

2 teaspoons chopped red seaweed (ogo; optional)

Julienned root vegetables, such as carrot, beet, and kohlrabi (optional)

Cut the tofu into 1-inch cubes. In a heatproof bowl, combine the boiling water, kosher salt, and tofu. Let it sit for 10 minutes, then drain and pat the tofu dry with a clean kitchen towel or paper towels. Dry the bowl. Return the tofu cubes to the bowl.

Add the soy sauce, sesame oil, Hawaiian salt, red onion, green onions, gochugaru, macadamia nuts, and seaweed (if using) and gently toss with your hands or a wooden spoon. Adjust the soy sauce and Hawaiian salt to taste. Cover the bowl and chill in the fridge for 30 minutes.

While the poke is chilling, soak the root veggies (if using) in an ice water bath. This will crisp them up. Drain and pat dry before using.

After the 30-minute chill, gently toss in the crisped veggies. Serve immediately.

Roasted Beet Poke

This may feel like a loose interpretation of poke since it features a roasted veggie, but don't forget what *poke* translates to! The zingy bright notes of ginger really bring this dish to life. If you don't have golden beets, you can absolutely use Chioggia or red beets. I find golden beets with their sunshiny color to be the sweetest, least earthy of beets, making them the perfect gateway beet for anyone who might be on the fence about this root veg. Roasting them caramelizes the natural sugars and enhances their flavor. If you can't find beets with their greens attached or in good condition, you can leave them out or substitute some dino (lacinato) kale or Swiss chard.

Serves 4

1½ pounds golden beets, peeled and cut into 1-inch pieces

2 tablespoons neutral oil (see page 18)

1 teaspoon kosher salt

1 teaspoon sugar

1 tablespoon toasted sesame seeds, ground

2 teaspoons toasted sesame oil

1 teaspoon rice vinegar

1 teaspoon finely grated peeled fresh ginger (½-inch knob)

½ teaspoon Hawaiian salt ('alaea)

5 green onions, green tops only, finely sliced on a bias

Handful of beet greens, chiffonade-cut

Preheat the oven to 350°F.

Place the beets on a sheet pan and drizzle with the neutral oil. Toss to coat the beets evenly. Sprinkle with the salt and toss again.

Roast until the beets are tender, 35 to 40 minutes, tossing and turning a couple of times while roasting.

When the beets are done, immediately toss them in the sugar on the sheet pan, then transfer them to a bowl. Add the sesame seeds, sesame oil, vinegar, ginger, Hawaiian salt, and green onion tops and gently toss with your hands or a wooden spoon. Adjust the seasoning to your liking.

You can serve this dish at room temperature or cover the bowl and let it chill in the fridge for 30 minutes. Serve topped with beet greens.

Watermelon Poke

Trust me when I say that you need to see and try this dish—watermelon poke is something to get excited about. It's a plan-ahead dish; you start it the day before you serve it, but it is worth making. The watermelon absorbs the marinade overnight, packing in the flavor while you sleep, and when it's cooked the next day, the texture is almost ʻahi (tuna)-like. The contrasting textures of the crunchy cucumber and creamy avocado play nicely with the meaty watermelon. Make this for your friends and family, but ask them to guess what it is. I'm willing to bet at least one person will guess it's ʻahi.

Serves 4

1 tablespoon rice vinegar

1 teaspoon fresh lemon juice

1½ tablespoons soy sauce (shoyu)

2 tablespoons toasted sesame oil

2 teaspoons extra-virgin olive oil

2 teaspoons honey

¼ teaspoon gochugaru (Korean chile flakes)

2 pounds seedless watermelon, rind removed, cut into 1-inch cubes

1 to 2 tablespoons neutral oil (see page 18), as needed

1 Persian (mini) cucumber, cut into ¾-inch lengths

¼ sweet onion, diced

1 avocado, cut into ¾-inch cubes

¼ teaspoon Hawaiian salt (ʻalaea)

1 tablespoon crushed toasted macadamia nuts

1 green onion, thinly sliced on a bias

In a large bowl, whisk together the vinegar, lemon juice, soy sauce, sesame oil, olive oil, honey, and gochugaru. Add the watermelon and gently toss to coat it evenly. Cover the bowl and refrigerate overnight.

In a large skillet, heat the neutral oil over medium heat until shiny. Transfer the cubed watermelon to the pan using a slotted spoon, shaking off as much marinade as possible into the bowl. (Don't discard the marinade. Transfer it to a container and reserve it in the refrigerator.) Cook the watermelon until it has dried out a bit and is a little caramelized around the edges, 5 to 6 minutes. Use a spatula to turn the watermelon to cook all sides evenly. Transfer the watermelon to a new bowl. Let it cool to room temperature before adding the cucumber and sweet onion, covering it and chilling it in the refrigerator for 2 hours.

When the watermelon is cold, remove it and the marinade from the refrigerator. Gently toss the avocado in the marinade and let it sit for 5 minutes before transferring it to the watermelon bowl using a slotted spoon. Sprinkle with the Hawaiian salt, macadamia nuts, and green onion and give everything a gentle toss to combine. Spoon on some marinade and serve immediately.

Tomato Poke

Make this dish at the height of summer using the best, sweetest tomatoes you can find. My not-so-humble brag is that the tomatoes you see in this dish came from our backyard garden! This poke celebrates the tomato by dressing it lightly with big hits of umami and a touch of sugar to enhance the tomatoes' sweetness. It's an unassuming side that truly shines; it's best served at room temperature but can also be chilled.

Serves 4

2 tablespoons soy sauce (shoyu)

1 tablespoon toasted sesame oil

1 tablespoon mirin

1 teaspoon sugar

1 garlic clove, finely grated

¼-inch piece fresh ginger, peeled and finely grated

1½ pounds tomatoes

2 Persian (mini) cucumbers or 1 Japanese cucumber

¼ red onion, thinly sliced

½ teaspoon Hawaiian salt (ʻalaea)

In a bowl, whisk together the soy sauce, sesame oil, mirin, sugar, garlic, and ginger until the sugar has dissolved.

Cut the tomatoes into 1-inch cubes (or cube-like pieces) and place them into the bowl. Halve the cucumber(s) lengthwise and then cut into ½-inch-thick half-moons and put into the bowl. Add the onion and Hawaiian salt and gently toss everything together using your hands so you don't bruise the tomatoes. Serve immediately.

sweets

Because there's always room (in life) for something sweet, these recipes are for adding a little extra treat to your meals. Whether it's a batch of butter mochi or a slice of Coconut Chiffon Cake (page 221), there are days when we could all use a pick-me-up or a celebratory dessert. This is the chapter for that. I tried to keep the serving sizes on these recipes down when I could. While I love a big pan of mochi for a potluck, I'd also like to be able to make a smaller batch to snack on throughout the week or to end a meal with friends. So most of these recipes are on the smaller serving size—with the Passion Fruit Chiffon Cake (page 223) as the exception, as I imagine you're not building a layer cake just to celebrate a Tuesday. If you are, this is a judgment-free zone, and I applaud this behavior. For all you sweet tooths, this one's for you—turn the page for a quick reference point for the local dishes that have inspired each subchapter. →

sweets

BUTTER MOCHI

This is a classic local Hawai'i dessert made with sweet rice flour (mochiko), eggs, milk, and of course, butter, that is bouncy, chewy, and slightly sticky. This subchapter explores new flavors for this uniquely Hawai'i baked mochi cake.

GURI GURI

Guri guri is a Hawai'i-style sherbet that originated on Maui. The recipes in this subchapter were built with home cooks in mind, so they are closer to a mix between guri guri and no-churn ice cream.

HAUPIA

Haupia is a classic Hawaiian dessert made with a few simple ingredients: coconut milk, milk, sugar, and cornstarch. It is sometimes referred to as "Hawaiian jello" or "Hawaiian pudding," though I'd say the creamy texture of this dish is closer to panna cotta.

CHIFFON CAKE

Light and airy chiffon cakes might not be what you think of when you think of local Hawai'i desserts, but they made their way over to the islands with the Japanese sugar and pineapple workers and are now mainstays. You'll find four ways to bake chiffon, from a traditional chiffon pan to a Bundt.

Kōloa, Kaua'i, Hawai'i Island

BUTTER MOCHI

Ube Butter Mochi

Butter mochi is a back-pocket kind of dessert. The classic Hawaiʻi version features a bouncy yet custardy interior with strong notes of butter and coconut, and the crust is crispy yet melty. Always the first thing to go on the dessert table, butter mochi is infinitely adaptable, leaving you with endless opportunities to stretch your creative legs. From ube (purple yam) to passion fruit (lilikoʻi), this smaller-batch recipe is bound to become your signature dessert. This recipe uses ube halaya jam—which is a purple yam jam that comes in a jar and can be found in many Asian markets and oftentimes in the Asian food aisle—and, optionally, ube flavoring to boost the signature notes of vanilla and sweet potato.

Makes 16 squares

Softened butter or oil, for the pan

2 large eggs, at room temperature

One 13.5-ounce can full-fat coconut milk

½ cup ube halaya jam

4 tablespoons (2 ounces/ ½ stick) unsalted butter, melted and cooled to room temperature

½ teaspoon ube flavoring (optional)

½ teaspoon vanilla extract

1¾ cups sweet rice flour (mochiko)

1 cup sugar

1 teaspoon baking powder

¼ teaspoon kosher salt

⅓ cup unsweetened coconut flakes

2 tablespoons unsweetened finely shredded coconut

Preheat the oven to 350°F. Grease an 8 by 8-inch baking pan with butter.

In a bowl, whisk together the eggs, coconut milk, ube halaya jam, melted butter, ube flavoring (if using), and vanilla. In a larger bowl, whisk together the sweet rice flour, sugar, baking powder, and salt. Pour the wet mixture into the dry mixture and whisk together until smooth and well combined. Ensure there aren't any clumps of mochiko in the batter and then pour into the prepared pan. Rap the pan on a kitchen towel set on the counter a few times until all air bubbles have surfaced.

Sprinkle the coconut flakes and shredded coconut on top and bake until the edges pull away from the pan's sides and the mochi is golden brown all over the top, including the center, about 1 hour.

Let cool completely in the pan on a wire rack before cutting the mochi into 16 squares. Store in an airtight container at room temperature for up to 3 days.

Passion Fruit Butter Mochi

My Aunty Darlyne and Uncle Terry inspired this recipe. They had an excess of passion fruit (liliko'i) and sent me a text to see whether it was possible to turn the butter mochi from *Aloha Kitchen* into passion fruit butter mochi. My response was "Absolutely," and it was so good that I had to include this smaller-batch recipe here in *Aloha Veggies*. If you're lucky enough to live in a place with lots of vines nearby, look for heavy fruit that's deeply the color of the outside (meaning dark yellow, red, or purple) when you're harvesting your passion fruit from the vine. I find the best fruit has already fallen and is starting to wrinkle. I cut my passion fruit in half, scoop out the pulp directly into my blender jar, then blend on low for no more than a minute to release the seeds. From there, I squeeze it through a nut milk bag, but you can leave the seeds in—they are edible and high in fiber. If you can't access fresh passion fruit, don't worry; you can usually find the pulp or concentrate frozen.

Makes 16 squares

Softened butter or oil, for the pan

2 large eggs, at room temperature

½ cup canned full-fat coconut milk

½ cup whole milk

½ cup passion fruit (liliko'i) concentrate, fresh or thawed frozen

4 tablespoons (2 ounces/ ½ stick) unsalted butter, melted and cooled to room temperature

1 teaspoon vanilla extract

1¾ cups sweet rice flour (mochiko)

1¼ cups sugar

1 teaspoon baking powder

¼ teaspoon kosher salt

¼ cup unsweetened finely shredded coconut

Preheat the oven to 350°F. Grease an 8 by 8-inch baking pan with butter.

In a bowl, whisk together the eggs, coconut milk, whole milk, passion fruit concentrate, melted butter, and vanilla. In a larger bowl, whisk together the sweet rice flour, sugar, baking powder, and salt. Pour the wet mixture into the dry mixture and whisk together until smooth and well combined. Ensure there aren't any clumps of mochiko in the batter and then pour into the prepared pan. Rap the pan on a kitchen towel set on the counter a few times until all air bubbles have surfaced.

Sprinkle the shredded coconut on top and bake until the edges pull away from the pan's sides and the mochi is golden brown all over the top, including the center, about 1 hour.

Let cool completely in the pan on a wire rack before cutting the mochi into 16 squares. Store in an airtight container at room temperature for up to 3 days.

Peanut Butter Marbled Mochi Brownies

Have you ever had a Reese's peanut butter cup? Maybe that's a silly question; let's assume you have. The peanut butter mixture swirled into these crackly-top mochi brownies resembles the peanut butter inside a Reese's PB cup. These are decidedly and intentionally on the drier side—I dare you to try a bite, if only to confirm!

Makes 16 squares

Brownie Mixture

Softened butter or oil, for the pan

2 large eggs, lightly beaten

6 tablespoons unsalted butter, melted and cooled to room temperature

1½ cups whole milk

1 teaspoon vanilla extract

1 cup sweet rice flour (mochiko)

1 cup granulated sugar

⅓ cup unsweetened cocoa powder

1½ teaspoons baking soda

½ teaspoon instant espresso powder (optional)

½ teaspoon kosher salt

4 ounces semisweet chocolate, chopped

Peanut Butter Mixture

⅓ cup smooth natural peanut butter

2 tablespoons unsalted butter, melted

1 tablespoon powdered sugar

½ teaspoon vanilla extract

Preheat the oven to 350°F. Grease an 8 by 8-inch baking pan with butter.

To make the brownie mixture: In a bowl, whisk together the eggs, melted butter, milk, and vanilla. In another larger bowl, whisk together the sweet rice flour, granulated sugar, cocoa powder, baking soda, espresso powder (if using), and salt. Pour the wet ingredients into the dry ingredients and whisk until smooth. Pour the mixture into the prepared pan. Rap the pan on a kitchen towel set on the counter a few times until all air bubbles have surfaced. Evenly sprinkle the chopped chocolate on the top.

To make the peanut butter mixture: In a bowl, mix the peanut butter, melted butter, powdered sugar, and vanilla with a spatula until smooth. If necessary, microwave the mixture 15 seconds at a time, until the mixture is warm enough to come together. Evenly spoon tablespoon-size dollops onto the top of the brownie mixture and gently swirl in with a knife. You want the peanut butter to be distributed throughout, with some peeking out on the top.

Bake until the edges pull away from the pan's sides and the mochi is golden brown all over the top, including the center, 1 hour 10 minutes to 1 hour 15 minutes. Insert a toothpick into the center to test doneness; it's done when it comes out clean or with a few little crumbs.

Let cool completely in the pan on a wire rack before cutting into 16 squares. Store in an airtight container at room temperature for up to 3 days.

Kabocha Butter Mochi

This is the coziest butter mochi I can think of. Perfect if you're looking for something to bake come fall but good enough that you'll want to bake it year-round. While I highly recommend making your kabocha puree because it's richer and nuttier than traditional canned pumpkin puree, I'll understand if you reach for a can. The recipe started with a can of pumpkin puree because one of my best friends, Kam Yai, requested pumpkin butter mochi. However, I just couldn't resist making a second batch with kabocha, and the rest is history.

Makes 16 squares

Softened butter or oil, for the pan

2 large eggs, at room temperature

½ cup roasted kabocha puree (see Note) or canned pumpkin puree

½ cup canned full-fat coconut milk

½ cup whole milk

4 tablespoons (2 ounces/ ½ stick) unsalted butter, melted and cooled to room temperature

1 teaspoon vanilla extract

1¾ cups sweet rice flour (mochiko)

1 cup plus 4 tablespoons sugar

1 teaspoon baking powder

2 teaspoons ground cinnamon

¾ teaspoon freshly grated nutmeg

¼ teaspoon kosher salt

¼ cup pumpkin seeds

Preheat the oven to 350°F. Grease an 8 by 8-inch baking pan with butter.

In a bowl, whisk together the eggs, kabocha puree, coconut milk, whole milk, melted butter, and vanilla. In a larger bowl, whisk together the sweet rice flour, 1 cup plus 2 tablespoons of the sugar, the baking powder, cinnamon, nutmeg, and salt. Pour the wet mixture into the dry mixture and whisk until smooth and well combined. Ensure there aren't any clumps of sweet rice flour in the batter and then pour into the prepared pan. Rap the pan on a kitchen towel set on the counter a few times until all air bubbles have surfaced.

Sprinkle on the pumpkin seeds and bake until the edges pull away from the pan's sides and the mochi is golden brown all over the top, including the center, about 1 hour. Immediately sprinkle on the remaining 2 tablespoons sugar.

Let cool completely in the pan on a wire rack before cutting into 16 squares. Store in an airtight container at room temperature for up to 3 days.

Note: To make roasted kabocha puree, preheat the oven to 425°F. Line a quarter-sheet pan with parchment paper. Rub the cut sides of a 1-pound wedge kabocha squash with 1 tablespoon extra-virgin olive oil and place cut-side down on the lined pan. Roast until the flesh is tender enough to pierce with a knife easily, 35 to 40 minutes. The cut side should be caramelized. Let it cool until it's cool enough to touch. Scoop the flesh from the skin and blend in a high-speed blender or food processor on low, scraping down the sides, until smooth. Let it cool completely before using.

O.K. Farms (Olsen Keolanui Farms)

Location
Hilo, Hawai'i Island, Hawai'i

Farm Stats
1,000 acres
9-foot elevation

Growing
Lychee, longan, cinnamon, heart of palm, citrus, cacao

Founded
2002

Owners
Edmund C. Olson Trust and Troy Keolanui

Our mission is to perpetuate sustainable agriculture in Hawai'i—feed the people!
—Kea Keolanui, daughter of Troy Keolanui

It feels like summer when your arms and hands are sticky from lychee's undeniably juicy, sweet flesh. Nowadays local lychee is harder and harder to find in Hawai'i, so when I discovered Kaimana (a variety) lychee from Hilo being sold at the grocery store in town, I did a double take. That's also how I discovered O.K. Farms. And the more I learned about the farm, the more interested I became. O.K. Farms is a lush and expansive farm just outside Hilo town, along the Wailuku River. They grow mainly tree crops that don't require any soil turnover, which is essential because, in the long run, they see it as more sustainable for the soil. With Hilo's wet climate, at least 130 inches of rain per year, trees like lychee, longan, and citrus thrive. Still, I was tickled to hear they've planted cinnamon trees! Local cinnamon!

Troy Keolanui and his family partnered with the late Edmund C. Olsen with a vision to keep the land green, abundant, and free from development. They envisioned a farm that could feed the people of Hawai'i. Today, they are a home for their community, a place where locals can visit and learn about where their food comes from. They host tours where the community can go, get their hands dirty, and participate in cultivating a locally sustainable future. The Keolanui family is striving to promote more local food consumption. They believe that the more independent Hawai'i can be regarding food, the better we will be as a community.

Strawberry Guri Guri

If you've visited Maui, chances are at least one person has told you to go to Tasaka Guri Guri in the Maui Mall. Created by Jokichi and Rise Tasaka in the early 1900s, guri guri is akin to sherbet, though it is its own thing. It was initially called "goodie goodie," but the name was mistaken for "guri guri," and it has remained. Today, the shop offers two flavors: strawberry and pineapple. The Tasaka family recipe for their very good guri guri is a closely guarded family treasure, and this isn't the grand recipe reveal. It is said that strawberry soda and maybe strawberry Jell-O could be some of the secret ingredients, but that's neither here nor there. I'm sharing my recipe for a more fruit-forward interpretation of the beloved frozen treat. Think of it as guri guri meets no-churn ice cream.

Makes about 4 cups

2 pounds fresh strawberries, hulled

Half a 14-ounce can sweetened condensed milk

½ cup heavy cream

1 tablespoon light corn syrup

1 teaspoon vanilla extract

½ teaspoon fresh lemon juice

⅛ teaspoon kosher salt

Chopped strawberries, for serving

In a high-powered blender or food processor, blend the strawberries until they are smooth. Strain through a fine-mesh sieve to remove the seeds and any remaining large particles. You should have about 1½ cups strawberry puree.

In a bowl, whisk the strawberry puree with the condensed milk, heavy cream, corn syrup, vanilla, lemon juice, and salt until smooth and well combined (see Note).

Transfer the mixture to a freezer-safe airtight container and freeze for 5 hours before serving. Halfway through the freezing process, remove the container and beat the mixture with a hand mixer or stand mixer on high for 2 to 3 minutes to break up some of the ice crystals forming. Return the mixture to the freezer.

If your guri guri is too hard to scoop, let it sit on the counter for a few minutes before scooping. Scoop and serve on its own or topped with chopped strawberries.

Note: If you have an ice cream machine, process the strawberry base according to your machine's instructions. You can serve it right after churning, and the texture will be closer to soft serve, or for a firmer texture, transfer the mixture to a freezer-safe, airtight container and freeze it for at least 4 hours before serving.

Ube Guri Guri

When I first made this ube (purple yam) guri guri, I left a batch in the freezer, and unbeknownst to me, Moses, my husband, helped himself to it. A few days went by, and out of nowhere, he said, "Hey, where'd you get that ube ice cream? It's good." The creamiest iteration of my recipes, this ube guri guri is so silky it might be mistaken for ice cream. Either way, it's pretty wonderful and so easy to make that you might find yourself filling your freezer with it! I highly recommend using it to make the Halo Halo with Haupia (page 218).

Makes about 4 cups

Half a 12-ounce jar ube halaya jam

Half a 13.5-ounce can full-fat coconut milk

Half a 14-ounce can sweetened condensed milk

½ cup heavy cream

1 tablespoon light corn syrup

½ teaspoon ube flavoring

⅛ teaspoon kosher salt

In a high-powered blender or food processor, blend the ube halaya jam, coconut milk, condensed milk, heavy cream, corn syrup, ube flavoring, and salt until smooth and well combined (see Note).

Transfer the mixture to a freezer-safe airtight container and freeze for 5 hours before serving. Halfway through the freezing process, remove the container and beat the mixture with a hand mixer or stand mixer on high for 2 to 3 minutes to break up some of the ice crystals forming. Return the mixture to the freezer.

If your guri guri is too hard to scoop, let it sit on the counter for a few minutes before scooping.

Note: If you have an ice cream machine, process the ube base according to your machine's instructions. You can serve it right after churning, and the texture will be closer to soft serve, or for a firmer texture, transfer the mixture to a freezer-safe, airtight container and freeze it for at least 4 hours before serving.

WATERMELON
UBE

Mango Guri Guri

There is nothing more glorious than mango season in Hawai'i, and with over sixty varieties, the season is pretty long, kicking off in May and winding down in October. I love mango in all forms, but having it ice cold on a hot summer day is pretty idyllic. This guri guri is all about the quality of mango, so try to use a sweet variety with a bit of tartness to balance out the creamy notes. Haden or Golden Glow are the two varieties I love the most.

Makes about 4 cups

1½ pounds mangoes, preferably Haden or Golden Glow, peeled and cubed, plus more for garnish

1 tablespoon water

Half a 14-ounce can sweetened condensed milk

½ cup heavy cream

1 tablespoon light corn syrup

½ teaspoon fresh lemon juice

⅛ teaspoon kosher salt

In a high-powered blender or food processor, blend the mango and the water until smooth. You should have about 1½ cups mango puree. It's okay if you have a little more or less. If you have a lot less, supplement with some liquid (water or milk, both work) and if you have a lot more, reserve the excess for a smoothie. Add the condensed milk, heavy cream, corn syrup, lemon juice, and salt and blend until smooth and well combined (see Note).

Transfer the mixture to a freezer-safe airtight container and freeze for 5 hours before serving. Halfway through the freezing process, remove the container and beat the mixture with a hand mixer or stand mixer on high for 2 to 3 minutes to break up some of the ice crystals forming. Return the mixture to the freezer.

If your guri guri is too hard to scoop, let it sit on the counter for a few minutes before scooping. Scoop and serve on its own or topped with chopped mango.

Note: If you have an ice cream machine, process the mango base according to your machine's instructions. You can serve it right after churning, and the texture will be closer to soft serve, or for a firmer texture, transfer the mixture to a freezer-safe, airtight container and freeze it for at least 4 hours before serving.

Watermelon Guri Guri

My other favorite place to get local Hawai'i-style sherbet is Asato Family, right off Pali Highway in downtown Honolulu. Neale Asato and his family are crafting some of the most exciting flavors of "local kine," meaning Hawai'i style, sherbet, like Piña Colada and White Rabbit (modeled after the candy). However, he does offer nostalgic favorites like strawberry and pineapple, which is a nod to Maui's Tasaka Guri Guri. As simple as this watermelon guri guri might sound on paper, the result is pretty magical. I feel like this creamy watermelon sherbet could be served at Asato Family with a drizzle of their famous li hing, (dried salted plum) sauce!

Makes about 4 cups

1 pound seedless watermelon flesh, chopped (about 3 cups)

Half a 14-ounce can sweetened condensed milk

½ cup heavy cream

1 tablespoon light corn syrup

½ teaspoon fresh lime juice

⅛ teaspoon kosher salt

Chopped watermelon and grated lime zest, for serving (optional)

In a high-powered blender or food processor, blend the watermelon until smooth. Strain through a fine-mesh sieve to remove any large particles. You should have about 1½ cups watermelon juice. If you have more, you can drink it; if you have less, supplement with additional liquid like water or milk.

In a bowl, whisk together the watermelon juice with the condensed milk, heavy cream, corn syrup, lime juice, and salt until smooth and well combined (see Note).

Transfer the mixture to a freezer-safe airtight container and freeze for 5 hours before serving. Halfway through the freezing process, remove the container and beat the mixture with a hand mixer or stand mixer on high for 2 to 3 minutes to break up some of the ice crystals forming. Return the mixture to the freezer.

If your guri guri is too hard to scoop, let it sit on the counter for a few minutes before scooping. Scoop and serve on its own or topped with chopped watermelon and some lime zest, if using.

Note: If you have an ice cream machine, process the watermelon base according to your machine's instructions. You can serve it right after churning, and the texture will be closer to soft serve, or for a firmer texture, transfer the mixture to a freezer-safe, airtight container and freeze it for at least 4 hours before serving.

Haupia Brownie

Yama's Fish Market in Honolulu, on the island of O'ahu, is where I fell in love with haupia brownies, though they call them "Brownie-licious Haupia Topped Brownies." Haupia, a classic Hawaiian dessert, is sometimes called coconut pudding, though it's closer to panna cotta or a creamy Jell-O. My haupia brownies are a little different than Yama's: They're intensely fudgy brownies topped with a thick layer of haupia. In essence, these have more haupia and less brownie; think a two-to-one ratio. I have found Aroy-D, Hawaiian Sun, and Chaokoh to be the best canned coconut milks for making haupia.

Makes 16 brownies

Brownie Layer

8 tablespoons (4 ounces/1 stick) unsalted butter

¾ cup packed light brown sugar

4 ounces semisweet chocolate, chopped

2 large eggs

1 teaspoon vanilla extract

¼ cup unsweetened cocoa powder

7 tablespoons all-purpose flour

½ teaspoon instant espresso powder

¾ teaspoon kosher salt

⅛ teaspoon baking soda

Haupia Layer

7 tablespoons granulated sugar

6 tablespoons cornstarch

¼ teaspoon kosher salt

One 13.5-ounce can full-fat coconut milk

¾ cup whole milk

Preheat the oven to 350°F. Line an 8 by 8-inch pan with parchment paper with excess on all sides to create "wings" that can be used to pull the brownies out later.

To make the brownie layer: In a saucepan, combine the butter and brown sugar and cook over medium heat, stirring a few times, until the butter starts to simmer. Remove from the heat and add the chocolate, stirring until the chocolate has melted. Pour into a bowl and set aside until cool enough to touch, 5 to 10 minutes.

To the bowl, add the eggs and vanilla and whisk together until the mixture is shiny and smooth, 2 to 3 minutes. Add the cocoa powder, flour, espresso powder, salt, and baking soda and mix with a spatula until all the flour has been incorporated. Pour the batter into the lined pan and use the spatula to smooth the surface. Rap the pan on a kitchen towel set on the counter a few times to get it evenly distributed.

Bake until the edges and top are set, 22 to 25 minutes. Set on a rack to cool.

To make the haupia layer: In a saucepan, whisk together the granulated sugar, cornstarch, and salt. Whisk in the coconut milk and whole milk and set over medium heat. Whisking constantly, cook until thickened, 6 to 8 minutes.

Immediately pour the haupia mixture over the brownies in an even layer, quickly smoothing the top with an offset spatula. Rap the pan on a kitchen towel set on the counter a few times to get it evenly distributed.

Refrigerate until the haupia is completely set, at least 2 hours. Cut into 16 squares and serve chilled.

Haupia Float

When I asked Moses, my partner, if he likes almond float, he responded, "Oh, yeah, I think my grandma used to make it." And in many ways, that speaks volumes; it is something your grandma used to make but doesn't get made often nowadays. But it's such a nice treat that I thought sharing this recipe might be a gentle reminder that it's excellent! Almond float was historically made with canned fruit cocktail, mandarins, and lychee. I wanted to provide a fresher take on it, but I kept the lychee with the syrup because it provides that core nostalgic flavor. While almond float is made with almond gelatin, haupia pairs well with the fresh fruits in this recipe. Give it a try; you won't be sorry!

Serves 4 to 6

2 kiwi, peeled and cut into bite-size wedges

¼ pineapple, peeled, cored, and cut into bite-size wedges

1 mango, preferably Haden or Golden Glow, peeled and cubed

One 20-ounce can lychees with syrup

¼ cup unsweetened coconut flakes, plus more for serving

Half an 8-inch-square pan Haupia (recipe follows), cut into ½-inch squares or diamonds

Flaky salt

In a bowl, combine the kiwi, pineapple, and mango. Pour the entire can of lychees, with the syrup, over the fruits. Cover the bowl and refrigerate for 1 hour.

In a small pan or skillet, toast the coconut flakes over medium heat, stirring, until fragrant and golden brown. The time will vary, so don't walk away; this happens quickly. Remove from the heat and set aside.

When you're ready to serve, add the haupia to the fruit bowl, tossing gently. To serve, spoon into bowls, adding some syrup to every bowl. Top with some coconut flakes and a sprinkle of flaky salt.

Haupia

Makes one 8-inch square pan

7 tablespoons sugar

6 tablespoons cornstarch

¼ teaspoon kosher salt

One 13.5-ounce can full-fat coconut milk

¾ cup whole milk

In a saucepan, whisk together the sugar, cornstarch, and salt. Whisk in the coconut milk and whole milk and set over medium heat. Whisking constantly, cook until thickened, 6 to 8 minutes. Immediately pour the mixture into an 8-inch-square baking pan, quickly smoothing the top with an offset spatula. Rap the pan on a kitchen towel set on the counter a few times to get it evenly distributed. Refrigerate for at least 2 to 3 hours or until the haupia is completely set.

Haupia French Toast

This is known as the "I-love-you French toast" in our house because I only make it for special occasions like birthdays or holidays. My husband jokes that I tricked him into falling in love with me because I made it more at the beginning of our relationship. I don't recall the history in the same way, but to each his/her own. At any rate, I'm not sure why I don't make it more often; it feels special without requiring a ton of effort. This recipe is inspired by the Halekulani Hotel's haupia French toast. I will date myself, but I think I probably had it fifteen, maybe twenty years ago. It was love at first bite, and now I know why my husband thinks I tricked him into falling in love with me.

Makes 4 slices

4 slices (1½ inches thick) milk bread, brioche, or sweet bread (see Note)

4 pieces (2¼ inches square) Haupia (page 214), cut in half

1¾ cups whole milk

4 large eggs

1 teaspoon vanilla extract

¼ teaspoon kosher salt

2 tablespoons unsalted butter

4 tablespoons unsweetened finely shredded coconut

4 teaspoons sugar

Sliced fresh fruit of your choice, for serving

Maple syrup, for serving

Using a sharp knife, make a pocket in the milk bread by cutting a slit through the top of the bread slices, through the center, being careful not to cut all the way through. Try to cut it as wide as possible without cutting through any of the sides. Repeat until all 4 slices have been cut. Carefully stuff each piece with a piece of haupia.

In a shallow bowl, whisk together the milk, eggs, vanilla, and salt.

In two batches, soak 2 pieces of bread in the egg mixture for anywhere from 10 seconds to 3 minutes on each side. You want your bread to be soaked but not soggy, and this will vary based on the type of bread you are using as well as how dry it is.

In a large skillet, heat 1 tablespoon of the butter over medium heat until it's melted, swirling the pan to distribute the butter. Shake off any excess egg mixture and place the 2 slices of stuffed bread in the pan. Sprinkle each slice with 1 tablespoon shredded coconut and 1 teaspoon sugar, in that order. Reduce the heat to medium-low, cover with a lid, and cook for 5 minutes. Flip, cover, and cook for another 5 minutes. Uncover, increase the heat to medium, and cook until golden brown, another 1 to 2 minutes. Repeat with the second batch.

Top with fruit and some maple syrup and serve.

Notes: Two- to three-day-old bread tends to work best. If you'd like to make this for dessert, top with a scoop of your favorite ice cream!

Halo Halo with Haupia

If you want to make someone's day, make them halo halo. It translates to "mix mix" in Tagalog, and the name says it all: You need to mix everything to combine all the layers of ingredients. There are many ways to make halo halo, but it's traditionally served with Filipino leche flan, not haupia. I think haupia is an excellent addition and pairs well with all the other ingredients. Since the haupia has to be chilled and set for this, plan ahead (refrigeration time is required). A jarred halo-halo fruit mix that consists of red mung bean, coconut strips, white bean, jackfruit pulp, and other ingredients in a sugar syrup makes prep a little easier, as there are many components, but you can customize and curate your mix. The easiest way to serve this is to get group participation and have everyone build their own!

Serves 4

One 12-ounce jar halo-halo fruit mix

4 cups shaved ice

½ cup evaporated milk

Sweetened condensed milk

1 mango, preferably Haden or Golden Glow, peeled and cubed

Ube ice cream or Ube Guri Guri (page 206)

4 pieces (2 inches square) Haupia (page 214), or cut into smaller pieces if desired

Collect 4 glasses, your choice of shape and size, but ideally aim for something that's around 8 ounces. Add about ⅓ cup halo-halo fruit mix (with syrup) to the bottom of each glass. Top each glass with around 1 cup of shaved ice. Drizzle 2 tablespoons of evaporated milk into each glass, then drizzle on sweetened condensed milk to taste (I usually add around 1 teaspoon). Top each glass with a few mango cubes, a scoop or two of ice cream or guri guri, and 1 haupia square.

Serve immediately with a spoon (a long one if you have a tall glass) and mix before enjoying.

Coconut Chiffon Cake

When I was maybe ten, I used to beg my mom to stop at Shirokiya, a Japanese store, at Ka'ahumanu Shopping Center in Kahului, Maui. The store must have had other items, but all I can remember is that it had Hello Kitty and chiffon cakes. I'm not sure, but I think they had four flavors of chiffon cakes, all baked in an angel food cake pan, so they had holes in the middle. The best part about these cakes was tearing the slice apart because it peeled in layers, so you could take your time and savor the fluffy, cloudlike cake. Shirokiya closed in 2001, and I've been dreaming about their chiffon cakes ever since. This coconut chiffon cake isn't one of their flavors, but the texture and pull-apart structure take me back to those days. If you're making the optional coconut topping, put two cans of coconut milk into your fridge the day before you plan on baking, as chilled, solidified coconut cream is a necessary component of the frosting.

Makes one 10-inch tube cake

Coconut Frosting (optional)

Two 13.5-ounce cans full-fat coconut milk

¼ cup mascarpone, softened at room temperature for 5 minutes

¼ cup powdered sugar

⅛ teaspoon kosher salt

Chiffon Cake

9 large eggs, separated

½ teaspoon cream of tartar

1¼ cups granulated sugar

¾ cup canned full-fat coconut milk

½ cup neutral oil (see page 18)

1½ teaspoons coconut extract

1½ cups cake flour

2 teaspoons baking powder

¾ teaspoon kosher salt

¼ cup unsweetened finely shredded coconut

To make the optional coconut frosting: Open both cans of coconut milk, trying not to shake or tilt the cans too much. Carefully scoop off the thick layer of solidified coconut cream on the top and place in a bowl. There should be a layer of coconut water on the bottom, which you should avoid adding to your cream. Save the coconut water for another use (I like to make smoothies with mine).

Add the mascarpone, powdered sugar, and salt and, using a hand mixer, whip it on high until soft peaks form, 1 to 2 minutes. Be careful not to overwhip, which can cause the mixture to separate. Cover the bowl and place in the refrigerator until you're ready to use it.

To make the chiffon cake: Preheat the oven to 350°F.

In a large bowl, with a hand mixer, combine the egg whites and cream of tartar and beat, starting on low speed and slowly working your way up to high speed, until nearly doubled in volume and very frothy, 1 to 2 minutes. Add 1 cup of the granulated sugar, ⅓ cup at a time, mixing after each addition for 30 seconds, reserving the remaining ¼ cup for later. Mix on high speed until glossy, stiff peaks form, 8 to 10 minutes. You can test the stiffness by stopping the mixer and pulling the beaters out of the bowl. If the mixture flops, it needs more time. If it holds its shape, it's stiff.

In another large bowl, combine the egg yolks and the remaining ¼ cup granulated sugar and beat on medium-high speed until well combined and slightly pale, about 2 minutes. Add the coconut milk, oil, and coconut extract and beat on medium speed until well combined.

Using a fine-mesh sieve, sift the flour, baking powder, and salt into the bowl with the egg yolk mixture. Mix with a silicone spatula until just combined. Add one-third of the egg white mixture and gently fold until just combined. Add the remainder of the egg white mixture and fold until there are no streaks of white.

Pour the batter into a 10-inch angel food cake pan. Rap the pan on a kitchen towel set on the counter several times to bring up any air bubbles.

Bake until the edges of the cake are just kissed with golden-brown color and the cake bounces back when you touch it, 30 to 40 minutes.

Flip the pan over onto the pan's legs (or a wire rack if your pan doesn't have

continued →

Coconut Chiffon Cake, continued

legs) and cool upside down until completely cool, about 3 hours.

Run a thin knife along the edges of the pan to release the cake. Carefully invert it onto a plate and use a knife to remove the bottom from the cake.

In a small pan or skillet, toast the shredded coconut over medium heat, stirring to evenly toast, until fragrant and golden brown. The time will vary, so don't walk away; this happens quickly. Remove from the heat and set aside.

Transfer the coconut frosting to a piping bag and pipe on the top of the cake as desired. Sprinkle the toasted coconut on top. Slice and serve. The coconut frosting will soften at room temperature, so this cake is best stored in the refrigerator, covered, for 2 to 3 days.

Passion Fruit Chiffon Cake

A layer cake might not be the first thing you think of when you think of chiffon, but they're a thing here in Hawai'i. You can find them at various bakeries around town, mostly on O'ahu, and yes, guava is likely the most well known. However, I think the bright, punchy flavors of passion fruit (liliko'i) are perfect for a layer cake. Each part of this cake is kissed with floral tang, from the chiffon to the mascarpone whipped cream to the glaze. There are a few steps to making this cake, but they can be broken up over a few different days. In fact, you can even freeze the cake layers and pull them out when you're ready to frost your cake.

Makes one 8-inch layer cake

Chiffon Cake

6 large eggs, separated

½ teaspoon cream of tartar

1¼ cups granulated sugar

½ cup passion fruit (liliko'i) concentrate, fresh or thawed frozen

5 tablespoons neutral oil (see page 18)

4 drops orange gel food coloring (optional)

1 cup cake flour

1¼ teaspoons baking powder

½ teaspoon kosher salt

Mascarpone Whipped Cream

6 cups heavy cream

2 cups mascarpone, softened at room temperature for 10 minutes

1 cup passion fruit (liliko'i) concentrate, fresh or thawed frozen

1½ cups powdered sugar

2 drops orange gel food coloring (optional)

¼ teaspoon kosher salt

Liliko'i Glaze

1 cup passion fruit (liliko'i) concentrate, fresh or thawed frozen

1½ cups granulated sugar

2½ tablespoons cornstarch

2 tablespoons cold water

To make the chiffon cake: Preheat the oven to 350°F. Line (only) the bottoms of two 8-inch round cake pans but do not grease the sides.

In a large bowl, with a hand mixer, combine the egg whites and cream of tartar and beat, starting on low speed and slowly working your way up to high speed, until nearly doubled in volume and very frothy, 1 to 2 minutes. Add 1 cup of the granulated sugar, ⅓ cup at a time, mixing after each addition for 30 seconds, reserving the remaining ¼ cup for later. Mix on high speed until glossy, stiff peaks form, 8 to 10 minutes. You can test the stiffness by stopping the hand mixer and pulling the beaters out of the bowl. If the mixture flops, it needs more time. If it holds its shape, it's stiff.

In another large bowl, combine the egg yolks and the remaining ¼ cup granulated sugar and beat on medium-high speed until well combined and slightly pale, about 2 minutes. Add the passion fruit concentrate, oil, and food coloring (if using) and beat on medium speed until well combined.

Using a fine-mesh sieve, sift the flour, baking powder, and salt into the bowl with the egg yolk mixture. Mix with a silicone spatula until just combined. Add one-third of the egg white mixture and gently fold until just combined. Add the remainder of the egg white mixture and fold until there are no streaks of white.

Divide the mixture between the lined cake pans and rap the pans on a kitchen towel set on the counter several times to bring up any air bubbles.

Bake until the edges of the cake are just kissed with golden-brown color, 20 to 24 minutes.

Remove the pans from the oven and set wire racks over the tops of the pans. Immediately flip over and cool upside down for 30 minutes to 1 hour, then run an offset spatula along the edges of the pans to release the cakes. Set the released cakes back on the rack to cool completely.

To make the mascarpone whipped cream: In a large bowl, combine the heavy cream, mascarpone, passion fruit concentrate, powdered sugar, food coloring (if using), and salt. Beat with a hand mixer, starting on low speed and working your way up to high speed, until stiff peaks form. Transfer half of the whipped cream to a piping bag fitted with a large round piping tip. Chill the bowl and the bag in the refrigerator until ready to use.

continued →

Passion Fruit Chiffon Cake, continued

To make the liliko'i glaze: In a small saucepan, combine the passion fruit concentrate and granulated sugar and bring to a high simmer over medium-high heat. In a small bowl, whisk together the cornstarch and cold water to create a slurry. Remove the pan from the heat and whisk in the slurry. Return the pan to the stovetop, set it over medium-low heat, and whisk continuously until it thickens slightly, 1 to 2 minutes. Pour the glaze into a bowl, cover with plastic wrap or something similar, and chill in the refrigerator for at least 30 minutes.

To assemble the cake, place one cake layer on a plate or cake stand and dollop half of the whipped cream from the bowl in the center of the cake. Pipe a border around the edge of the cake and then use an offset spatula to spread the cream evenly to the edges. Place the second layer of cake on top, pressing it gently to secure it. Dollop the remaining half of the whipped cream in the bowl in the center of the cake and use your offset spatula to spread it across the top and down the sides. Aim to coat the entire cake in a thin layer of whipped cream. Transfer the cake to the refrigerator for 10 minutes to firm up.

Pipe a few rings of whipped cream around the cake and use the offset spatula to smooth it out. Pipe a decorative ring around the top of the cake; this will serve as decoration and a border for the glaze. Spoon on the glaze and use a clean offset spatula to gently spread it into an even layer. This cake can be stored in the refrigerator, covered, for up to 3 days.

Guava Chiffon Roll

The whimsy of a roll cake just gets me. This roll is airy and subtly sweet but packed with guava flavor. The slice-and-eat aspect speaks to me, as someone who often wants a sweet treat but doesn't always want a full production. You can cut a few slices to take on the go, or serve it up with some afternoon tea.

Makes 1 roll

Chiffon Cake

6 large eggs, separated

½ teaspoon cream of tartar

¾ cup granulated sugar

½ cup guava concentrate (see Note)

5 tablespoons neutral oil (see page 18)

4 drops pink gel food coloring (optional)

1 cup cake flour

1¼ teaspoons baking powder

½ teaspoon kosher salt

Mascarpone Whipped Cream

1½ cups heavy cream

½ cup mascarpone, softened at room temperature for 5 minutes

½ cup powdered sugar

¼ cup guava concentrate (see Note)

1 to 2 drops pink gel food coloring (optional)

⅛ teaspoon kosher salt

To make the chiffon cake: Preheat the oven to 350°F. Line (only) the bottom of an 18 by 13-inch half-sheet pan but do not grease the sides.

In a large bowl, with a hand mixer, combine the egg whites and cream of tartar and beat, starting on low speed and slowly working your way up to high speed, until nearly doubled in volume and very frothy, 1 to 2 minutes. Add ½ cup of the granulated sugar, ¼ cup at a time, mixing after each addition for 30 seconds, reserving the remaining ¼ cup for later. Mix on high speed until glossy, stiff peaks form, 8 to 10 minutes. You can test the stiffness by stopping the hand mixer and pulling the beaters out of the bowl. If the mixture flops, it needs more time. If it holds its shape, it's stiff.

In another large bowl, combine the egg yolks and the remaining ¼ cup granulated sugar and beat on medium-high speed until well combined and slightly pale, about 2 minutes. Add the guava concentrate, oil, and food coloring (if using) and beat on medium speed until well combined.

Using a fine-mesh sieve, sift the flour, baking powder, and salt into the bowl with the egg yolk mixture. Mix with a silicone spatula until just combined. Add one-third of the egg white mixture and gently fold until just combined. Add the remainder of the egg white mixture and fold until there are no streaks of white.

Pour the batter into the lined half-sheet pan. Rap the pan on a kitchen towel set on the counter several times to bring up any air bubbles.

Bake until the edges of the cake are just kissed with golden-brown color, 12 to 14 minutes.

Remove the pan from the oven and let the cake cool for 5 minutes before running an offset spatula along the edges of the pan to release the cake. Place a clean kitchen towel on top of the cake followed by a wire rack and, with hands on both ends, flip the pan over. Remove the pan and peel off the parchment paper. Place another clean kitchen towel over the top and flip the cake again. Remove the first towel and begin rolling the cake, from a short end. Let the cake cool in this rolled shape.

To make the mascarpone whipped cream: In a bowl, using a hand mixer, combine the heavy cream, mascarpone, powdered sugar, guava concentrate, food coloring (if using), and salt. Beat, starting on low speed and working your way up to high speed, until stiff peaks form.

Carefully unroll the cake and, leaving a 1½-inch margin at the end, smooth on an even layer of whipped cream. Roll the cake back up, ending with the side with the margin. Wrap the cake in plastic wrap and chill for at least 2 hours before slicing. Trim the ends, if desired, then slice into 1-inch slices and serve. Store in the refrigerator for 3 days.

Note: This recipe uses guava concentrate, which is easy to make at home. To make it, boil 64 ounces of guava nectar (I used Sun Tropics) over high heat until reduced by two-thirds. This takes 30 to 40 minutes.

Lime Chiffon Loaf Cake

This loaf is perfect for the days when you want some cake for breakfast or with some tea in the afternoon. Pillowy soft, bright, and fresh, this sliceable chiffon is so satisfying that you'll find yourself cutting another slice in no time.

Makes one 9 by 5-inch loaf

6 large eggs, separated

½ teaspoon cream of tartar

1 cup granulated sugar

Grated zest of ½ lime

2 tablespoons fresh lime juice

¼ teaspoon lime extract

6 tablespoons whole milk

5 tablespoons neutral oil (see page 18)

4 to 6 drops green gel food coloring (optional)

1 cup cake flour

1½ teaspoons baking powder

½ teaspoon kosher salt

Powdered sugar, for serving

Preheat the oven to 350°F. Line (only) the bottom of a 9 by 5-inch loaf pan but do not grease the sides.

In a large bowl, with a hand mixer, combine the egg whites and cream of tartar and beat, starting on low speed and slowly working your way up to high speed, until nearly doubled in volume and very frothy, 1 to 2 minutes. Add ¾ cup of the sugar, ¼ cup at a time, to the egg whites, mixing after each addition for 30 seconds, reserving the remaining ¼ cup for later. Mix on high speed until glossy, stiff peaks form, 8 to 10 minutes. You can test the stiffness by stopping the hand mixer and pulling the beaters out of the bowl. If the mixture flops, it needs more time. If it holds its shape, it's stiff.

In another large bowl, with a hand mixer, combine the egg yolks, the remaining ¼ cup sugar, and the lime zest and beat on medium-high speed until well combined and slightly pale, about 2 minutes. Add the lime juice, lime extract, milk, oil, and food coloring (if using) and beat on medium speed until well combined.

Using a fine-mesh sieve, sift the flour, baking powder, and salt into the bowl with the egg yolk mixture. Mix with a silicone spatula until just combined. Add one-third of the egg white mixture and gently fold until just combined. Add the remainder of the egg white mixture and fold until there are no streaks of white.

Pour the batter into the lined loaf pan. Rap the pan on a kitchen towel set on the counter several times to bring up any air bubbles.

Bake until the edges of the cake are just kissed with golden-brown color and the top springs back when you press it, 30 to 40 minutes.

Remove the pan from the oven and set a wire rack over the top of the pan. Immediately flip over and cool upside down for 30 minutes, then run an offset spatula along the edges of the pan to release the cake. Set the released cake back on the rack to cool completely.

To serve, dust with powdered sugar and slice. Store covered, at room temperature, for up to 3 days.

complete meal matrix

This section is designed for the days when you're unsure what to make. Here's the plan: Pick a main flavor or technique you're in the mood for; maybe it's huli huli or jun. Find that subchapter and then take a look at all the starches and sides that go well with them. From there, you can narrow down a specific recipe from each chapter to build your complete meal.

Main + Starch + Side = A Complete Meal

mains

SHOYU	Shoyu Cauliflower with Chickpeas (p. 25)
	Shoyu Kabocha with Green Onion Oil and Whipped Tofu (p. 26)
	Shoyu-Roasted Carrots with Butter Bean Puree (p. 29)
	Shoyu Japanese Turnips with Oyster Mushrooms and Bok Choy (p. 30)
KATSU	Globe Eggplant Katsu (p. 33)
	Potato Cake Katsu with Curry (p. 34)
	Tofu Wasabi Pea Katsu (p. 37)
	Kohlrabi Steak Arare Katsu (p. 38)
HULI HULI	Huli Huli Zucchini with Crispy Chickpeas (p. 41)
	Huli Huli Tofu with Watercress (p. 42)
	Huli Huli Cauliflower Steaks with Cauliflower Puree (p. 45)
	Huli Huli Hasselback Butternut Squash (p. 46)
MISO	Miso Cabbage with Oyster Mushrooms (p. 49)
	Miso Beets with Cannellini Beans (p. 50)
	Roasted Miso Sweet Potato with Pumpkin Seeds (p.53)
	Braised Miso Eggplant (p. 54)
LAULAU	Sweet Potato, Mushroom, Onion, and Garlic Laulau (p. 58)
	Breadfruit, Kabocha, and Ginger Laulau (p. 58)
	Carrot, Turnip, Beet, Onion, Garlic, and Ginger Laulau (p. 58)
	Taro, Sweet Potato, Daikon, and Garlic Laulau (p. 58)
BEAN SOUP	Hearty Veggie Portuguese Bean Soup (p. 64)
	Shiitake and Bok Choy with Chickpea Soup (p. 66)
	Watercress and Corn with White Bean Soup (p. 69)
	Squash and Pinto Bean Soup (p. 70)
LOCO MOCO	Tofu Burgers Loco Moco (p. 72)
	Black Bean Mushroom Burgers Loco Moco (p. 74)
	Breadfruit White Bean Burgers Loco Moco (p. 77)
	Black Lentils Burger Loco Moco (p.78)

starches

MIXED RICE				FRIED RICE				CRISPY RICE				MASH			
Mushroomy Rice (p. 130)	Choy Sum Rice (p. 134)	Edamame Rice (p. 137)	Azuki Bean Rice (p. 138)	Garlicky Green Bean Fried Rice (p. 141)	Ginger Cabbage Fried Farro (p. 142)	Shiitake and Kale Fried Quinoa (p. 145)	Kimchi Carrot Fried Rice (p. 146)	Pan-Seared Crispy Rice (p. 148)	Rice Crispies (p. 149)	Quinoa Crispies (p. 150)	Farro Crispies (p. 151)	Coconut Sweet Potato Mash (p. 153)	Kabocha Mash (p. 154)	Taro Mash (p. 157)	Garlicky Breadfruit Mash (p. 158)
●	●		●					●				●	●	●	●
●	●	●	●						●	●	●				
●	●		●		●	●		●	●	●	●				
●	●		●					●				●	●	●	●
●	●	●	●				●	●					●	●	●
●			●					●							
●	●	●	●				●	●					●		
●	●	●	●				●	●					●	●	●
●	●	●	●	●	●	●	●	●				●	●	●	●
●	●	●	●	●	●	●	●	●	●	●	●	●	●	●	●
●	●	●	●	●	●	●	●	●	●	●	●				
●	●	●	●	●	●	●	●	●	●	●	●	●	●	●	●
●	●	●	●	●	●	●	●	●	●	●	●	●	●	●	●
●	●	●	●	●	●	●	●	●	●	●	●	●	●	●	●
●	●	●	●	●	●	●	●	●							
●	●	●	●	●	●	●	●	●	●	●	●	●	●	●	●
●	●		●					●				●	●	●	●
●	●		●					●				●	●	●	●
●	●		●					●				●	●	●	●
●	●		●					●				●	●	●	●
	●		●						●	●	●				
	●		●						●	●	●				
	●		●						●	●	●				
	●		●						●	●	●				
●	●			●	●	●	●								
●	●			●	●	●	●								
●	●			●	●	●	●								
●	●			●	●	●	●								

sides

QUICKLE				SALAD				POTATO MAC SALAD				POKE			
Everyday Quickle (p. 164)	Quick Kimchi Zucchini (p. 165)	Quick Namasu (p. 166)	Shoyu Onion Quickle (p. 167)	Tofu Watercress Salad (p. 169)	Shaved Brussels Sprout and Cabbage Salad (p. 170)	Kale and Shoyu Mushroom Salad (p. 173)	Corn and Avocado Salad (p. 174)	Namasu Sweet Potato Salad (p. 177)	Breadfruit Mac Salad (p. 178)	Kabocha Potato Salad (p. 182)	Kimchi Taro Mac Salad (p. 183)	Tofu Poke (p. 185)	Roasted Beet Poke (p. 186)	Watermelon Poke (p. 189)	Tomato Poke (p. 190)
●	●	●		●	●		●	●	●	●	●	●	●	●	●
●	●	●	●	●	●	●	●	●	●	●	●	●	●	●	●
●	●	●	●	●	●	●	●					●	●	●	●
●	●	●		●	●	●	●	●	●	●	●	●	●	●	●
●	●	●	●	●	●	●	●	●	●	●	●	●	●	●	●
●		●	●	●	●	●	●	●	●	●		●	●	●	●
●		●	●	●	●	●	●	●	●	●		●	●	●	●
●	●	●	●	●	●	●	●	●	●	●	●	●	●	●	●
●	●	●	●	●	●	●	●	●	●	●	●	●	●	●	●
●	●	●	●		●	●	●	●	●	●	●	●	●	●	●
●	●	●	●	●	●	●	●	●	●	●	●	●	●	●	●
●	●	●	●	●	●	●	●	●	●	●	●	●	●	●	●
●	●	●	●					●	●	●	●	●	●	●	●
●	●	●	●					●	●	●	●	●	●	●	●
●	●	●	●					●	●	●	●	●	●	●	●
●	●	●	●					●	●	●	●	●	●	●	●
●	●	●	●					●	●	●	●	●	●	●	●
●	●	●	●					●	●	●	●	●	●	●	●
●	●	●	●					●	●	●	●	●	●	●	●
●	●	●	●					●	●	●	●	●	●	●	●
				●	●	●	●								
				●	●	●	●								
				●	●	●	●								
				●	●	●	●								
				●	●	●	●		●		●				
				●	●	●	●		●		●				
				●	●	●	●		●		●				
				●	●	●	●		●		●				

continued →

complete meal matrix, continued

Main + Starch + Side = A Complete Meal

mains

ADOBO	Cabbage Adobo with Butternut Squash and Black Lentils (p. 81)
	Japanese Eggplant "Adobo" (p. 82)
	Daikon Adobo (p. 85)
	Long Bean Adobo with Oyster Mushrooms and Abura-age (p. 89)
MOCHIKO	Classic Mochiko (p. 90)
	Make it Sesame-y! (p. 91)
	Make it Gingery! (p. 91)
	Make it Spicy! (p. 91)
JUN	Green Bean Jun (p. 95)
	Zucchini Jun (p. 96)
	Yuba, Cabbage, and Sweet Potato Jun (p. 99)
	Oyster Mushroom Jun (p. 100)
CHINESE-STYLE	Soft Tofu with Watercress Chinese-Style (p. 103)
	Broccolini Chinese-Style (p. 107)
	Roasted Eggplant with Macadamia Nuts Chinese-Style (p. 108)
	Sugar Snap Peas Chinese-Style (p. 111)
LŪ'AU STEW	Sweet Potato and Black Bean Lū'au Stew (p.112)
	Swiss Chard Lū'au Stew with Japanese Turnips and Black Lentils (p. 115)
	Cremini Ginger Lū'au Stew with Shoyu Mushrooms (p. 116)
	Spinach Lū'au Stew with Sesame-Crusted Tofu (p. 119)
FURIKAKE	Furikake-Roasted Cauliflower (p. 120)
	Furikake-Broiled Eggplant (p. 122)
	Spicy Mayo Roasted Honeynut Squash (p. 123)
	Dynamite Portabello (p. 125)

starches

	MIXED RICE				FRIED RICE				CRISPY RICE				MASH			
	Mushroomy Rice (p. 130)	Choy Sum Rice (p. 134)	Edamame Rice (p. 137)	Azuki Bean Rice (p. 138)	Garlicky Green Bean Fried Rice (p. 141)	Ginger Cabbage Fried Farro (p. 142)	Shiitake and Kale Fried Quinoa (p. 145)	Kimchi Carrot Fried Rice (p. 146)	Pan-Seared Crispy Rice (p. 148)	Rice Crispies (p. 149)	Quinoa Crispies (p. 150)	Farro Crispies (p. 151)	Coconut Sweet Potato Mash (p. 153)	Kabocha Mash (p. 154)	Taro Mash (p. 157)	Garlicky Breadfruit Mash (p. 158)
	●	●		●	●	●	●	●	●	●	●	●	●	●	●	●
	●	●		●	●	●	●	●	●	●	●	●	●	●	●	●
	●	●		●	●	●	●	●	●	●	●	●	●	●	●	●
	●	●		●	●	●	●	●	●	●	●	●	●	●	●	●
	●	●	●	●	●	●	●	●	●				●	●	●	●
	●	●	●	●	●	●	●	●	●				●	●	●	●
	●	●	●	●	●	●	●	●	●				●	●	●	●
	●	●	●	●	●	●	●	●	●				●	●	●	●
	●	●		●	●	●	●	●	●				●	●	●	●
	●	●		●	●	●	●	●	●				●	●	●	●
	●	●		●	●	●	●	●	●				●	●	●	●
	●	●		●	●	●	●	●	●				●	●	●	●
	●	●		●					●							
	●	●		●					●							
	●	●		●					●							
	●	●		●					●		●					
													●			●
													●			●
													●			●
													●			●
			●													
			●													
			●													
			●													

sides

	QUICKLE				SALAD				POTATO MAC SALAD				POKE			
	Everyday Quickle (p. 164)	Quick Kimchi Zucchini (p. 165)	Quick Namasu (p. 166)	Shoyu Onion Quickle (p. 167)	Tofu Watercress Salad (p. 169)	Shaved Brussels Sprout and Cabbage Salad (p. 170)	Kale and Shoyu Mushroom Salad (p.173)	Corn and Avocado Salad (p. 174)	Namasu Sweet Potato Salad (p. 177)	Breadfruit Mac Salad (p. 178)	Kabocha Potato Salad (p. 182)	Kimchi Taro Mac Salad (p. 183)	Tofu Poke (p. 185)	Roasted Beet Poke (p. 186)	Watermelon Poke (p. 189)	Tomato Poke (p. 190)
	●	●	●	●					●	●	●	●	●	●		●
	●	●	●	●					●	●	●	●	●	●		●
	●	●	●	●					●	●	●	●	●	●		●
	●	●	●	●					●	●	●	●	●	●		●
	●	●	●	●	●	●	●	●	●	●	●	●	●	●	●	●
	●	●	●	●	●	●	●	●	●	●	●	●	●	●	●	●
	●	●	●	●	●	●	●	●	●	●	●	●	●	●	●	●
	●	●	●	●	●	●	●	●	●	●	●	●	●	●	●	●
	●	●	●	●	●			●	●	●	●	●	●	●		●
	●	●	●	●	●			●	●	●	●	●	●	●		●
	●	●	●	●	●			●	●	●	●	●	●	●		●
	●	●	●	●	●			●	●	●	●	●	●	●		●
													●	●		●
													●	●		●
													●	●		●
													●	●		●
				●												
				●												
				●												
				●												
	●	●	●	●	●	●	●	●	●	●	●	●	●	●	●	●
	●	●	●	●	●	●	●	●	●	●	●	●	●	●	●	●
	●	●	●	●	●	●	●	●	●	●	●	●	●	●	●	●
		●	●	●	●	●	●	●	●	●	●	●	●	●	●	●

Sumida Farm, Aiea, ʻOahu

me ka mahalo piha
with a fullness of gratitude

This book would not exist without the patience, love, and endless support of my family and friends.

As much as I'd like to pretend that living with a cookbook author is awesome, it's admittedly less glamorous than it might seem. Thank you to my husband, Moses, for learning to navigate gracefully around the constant exclamations of "No, I need those green onions," or "Please don't put my pan away; I'm using it for a recipe later today, or maybe tomorrow . . ." I appreciate you letting me turn our upstairs into a photo studio for over a year and for acting as an unofficial dishwasher during that time. Incredible doesn't feel like an adequate way to describe your art direction and brilliant veggie Hawaiian quilt-inspired artwork; I don't know how you found the time to make this book what it is, but I feel lucky that you did.

To my parents, I am immeasurably grateful for the lessons and tools you instilled in me, despite my many vocal protests throughout the years early on. Dad, you can tell your friends you helped write this book if you want. A special thank-you to my mom for her mother's intuition, always showing up with meals when they were needed most.

To my publisher, Ten Speed Press, and the extraordinary team that brought this book to life, I feel so lucky to have collaborated with all of you. Working with you has always been a dream. To Kelly Snowden, I won the lottery working with you on *Aloha Kitchen.* I'm forever grateful for your gentle guidance and flexibility throughout this journey of *Aloha Veggies.* I love your love for Hawai'i, and I can never thank you enough for always championing my voice. Gabby Ureña Matos, mahalo for your enthusiasm and positive energy. Abby Oladipo, your quiet presence did not go unnoticed. Kate Slate, I appreciated every one of your copyedits—you made the book much stronger than it was; thank you. Annie Marino and Mari Gill, without you, this book wouldn't have been half of what it is. Thank you for lending your creative magic to *Aloha Veggies.*

To the marketing, publicity, and sales teams, thanks for seeing and sharing this book's love of veggies with readers near and far.

Nicole Tourtelot, knowing you're in my corner makes me feel like I can do almost anything. Thank you for believing in me and understanding my vision of what *Aloha Veggies* could be from the start.

To the friends who have checked in on me throughout the process of making this book, offered to test a recipe, or sometimes taste a recipe, my sanity and I thank you. Lily Diamond, you sure know how to make a person feel seen and loved. Because of you, there's a book two (and one, if we're honest). Tash, you are everyone's dream cheerleader, and your exuberant energy carried me through a few of the more challenging days. To the Paschers, thank you for sharing so much of your backyard bounty with me; everything you grow is truly a gift.

To all the stewards of the land, with extra aloha to Kāko'o 'Ōiwi, Lapa'au Farm, O.K. Farms, Noho'ana Farm, and Sumida Farm, my heart is full of gratitude to you for all that you do. Feeding the people of Hawai'i, striving to provide food security for future generations, building community, preserving history and culture, and restoring the vitality of the land, I (we all) see you. I'm officially part of each of your fan clubs and will continue to support you in any way I can.

To the weenies, Miso, Hina, and my sweet heavenly Vienna. You are the best friends and little balls of love and light a girl could ask for.

To you, the reader, I am so happy and honored that you've joined me on this exploration of veggies and local Hawai'i food. I loved creating this book and hope it finds a good spot in your kitchen, on your bookshelf, or on your coffee table. Cheers to spending more joyful time in the kitchen.

Aloha,

Alana

index

TEN SPEED PRESS
An imprint of the Crown Publishing Group
A division of Penguin Random House LLC
1745 Broadway
New York, NY 10019
tenspeed.com
penguinrandomhouse.com

Typefaces: Linotype's Helvetica Now and Latinotype's Goldplay

Library of Congress Cataloging-in-Publication Data
Names: Kysar, Alana, 1985- author photographer
Title: Aloha veggies : veg-forward recipes celebrating the flavors of Hawai'i / by Alana Kysar ; photography by Alana Kysar.
Identifiers: LCCN 2025025727 (print) | LCCN 2025025728 (ebook) | ISBN 9780593836194 hardcover | ISBN 9780593836200 ebook
Subjects: LCSH: Hawaiian cooking | Vegetarian cooking | Cooking (Vegetables) | LCGFT: Cookbooks
Classification: LCC TX724.5.H3 K975 2026 (print) | LCC TX724.5.H3 (ebook) | DDC 641.5/63609969--dcundefined
LC record available at https://lccn.loc.gov/2025025727
LC ebook record available at https://lccn.loc.gov/2025025728

Hardcover ISBN: 978-0-593-83619-4
Ebook ISBN: 978-0-593-83620-0

Editor: Kelly Snowden | Production editor: Abby Oladipo
Editorial assistant: Gabby Ureña Matos
Art director, designer, and artwork: Moses Aipa
Production designers: Annie Marino, Mari Gill, and Faith Hague
Production: Jane Chinn
Food and prop stylist: Alana Kysar
Copy editor: Kate Slate | Proofreaders: Heather Rodino, Penelope Haynes, Andrea Peabbles, and Nicole Ramirez | Indexer: Thérèse Shere
Publicist: Kristin Casemore | Marketer: Andrea Portanova

Manufactured in China

10 9 8 7 6 5 4 3 2 1

First Edition

The authorized representative in the EU for product safety and compliance is Penguin Random House Ireland, Morrison Chambers, 32 Nassau Street, Dublin D02 YH68, Ireland, https://eu-contact.penguin.ie.

Kula, Maui

SQUASH  MUSHROOM  CARROT  EGGPLANT  WATERCRESS

SOYBEAN  PASSION FRUIT  CAULIFLOWER  SWEET POTATO  RICE

CITRUS

QUILT PATTERNS

Iconic Hawaiian quilts are recognized worldwide for their bold and beautiful patterns, often inspired by the natural world. The veggie-focused, Hawaiian quilt-inspired artwork in this book pays homage to Hawai'i's diverse creative heritage.

BREADFRUIT

TARO  TOMATO  WATERMELON  COCONUT CABBAGE